Praise for *Leading Equity*

"Dr. Sheldon Eakins has written a masterpiece! The topic of equity is by far the hottest topic in education today. Countless educators are writing about equity inclusive of what it is and what it is not. In *Leading Equity*, Dr. Eakins has gone beyond theory. This book is introducing ten actionable steps that a teacher can implement in the classroom immediately. At the proverbial end of the day, this is what teachers are looking for – strategies and solutions that they can take immediate hold of."
—Baruti K. Kafele, Retired Principal,
Education Consultant, Author

"When I think of people who are leading the way in the work of Equity, Sheldon Eakins immediately comes to mind. *Leading Equity* is the book I wish I would have had when I began my career in education. It is thought provoking, moving, and helps the reader grow into a better human and educator. This should be required reading for anyone working with kids."

—Todd Nesloney,
Director of Culture and Strategic Leadership at TEPSA,
bestselling author, international speaker

"Dr. Sheldon Eakins' *Leading Equity* book is the culturally responsive actionable guide that every teacher needs! Stemming from his impressive scholar/practitioner background, it engages critical topics like asset-based pedagogy, decolonizing the classroom, acknowledging privileges/biases and embracing humility and discomfort with lesson plans, case studies, and prompts for all to engage and apply. It is comprehensive in scope and relentlessly committed to more just classrooms, schools, and societies."

—**Emily Affolter**, Ph.D.,
Prescott College Faculty in Sustainability Education

"*Leading Equity* is a must read for educators and school leaders. Amidst so much controversy and politicization, it's easy to forget how vital questions of identity are to ensuring equitable and positive schooling outcomes, yet Sheldon Eakin's text invites us in accessible, welcoming ways to consider how we can help students navigate the complicated terrain of race, identity and culture in classrooms, while supporting educators to reflect productively on our own identities and responsibilities in the classroom. This is a real contribution to how we approach our diverse classrooms in the present era."

—**Michael C. Domínguez**,
Associate Professor of Chicana and Chicano Studies,
San Diego State University

"Dr. Eakins takes us on a profound journey of self-reflection and improvement, weaving together real-life stories and practical reflection activities to help us recognize and understand our privileges and biases. Sheldon guides us through the often uncomfortable admission that is necessary for us to embrace the challenge of self-reflection so we can better understand, connect with, and support our students, colleagues, and community members."

—**Jeff Gargas**,
COO/Co-Founder, Teach Better Team

"*Leading Equity* by Sheldon Eakins is an evergreen AND relevant book 'for the times' as it accomplishes inclusivity and access for all educators, including equity skeptics! In the opening paragraph of chapter one, Sheldon isn't shy about addressing the elephant in the room—instead, he writes, 'Sometimes, when we hear the word *privilege*, we default to the popular term, *White privilege*. The reality is, though, we all have some form of privilege.' I appreciate his honesty for colleagues who already understand this but are made to feel otherwise. In current troubling times, teaching teams need warm and truthful feedback—we also need to learn how to be inclusive and collegial to raise equity for vulnerable students. Through the powerful reflective activities found in this book, Sheldon expertly provides what schools need to begin and sustain equity efforts!"

—Jorge Valenzuela,
Education Coach, Author and Advocate

Leading Equity

Leading Equity

Becoming an Advocate for All Students

Sheldon L. Eakins, PhD

WILEY

Jossey-Bass
A Wiley Imprint
111 River St, Hoboken, NJ 07030
www.josseybass.com

Simultaneously published in Canada

Library of Congress Cataloging-in-Publication Data is Available:

ISBN 9781119840978 (paperback)
ISBN 9781119840992 (ePDF)
ISBN 9781119840985 (ePub)

COVER DESIGN: PAUL MCCARTHY
COVER ART: © GETTY IMAGES / KLAUS VEDFELT
AUTHOR PHOTO: © SHELON EAKINS

FIRST EDITION

SKY10034629_060122

This book is dedicated to all the educators who continue to go above and beyond the call for their students despite everything happening within their personal and professional lives.

Contents

Preface

And what did you do?

—Anonymous

I have spent a lot of time thinking about what it means to be an advocate. It is a concept that I find intriguing as many of us have different thoughts regarding what it means. An advocate recognizes that we do not live in a just society. Advocates are not satisfied with the status quo and are willing to speak up on behalf of others. I know it sounds good on paper, and I do not say this to you as if I have always been on my game when it comes to doing advocacy work in education. I've made mistakes; I've missed opportunities; I'm not flawless in my approach because many situations I have faced have caught me off guard and have left me without the words or mental preparation to respond. I believe we are all on a journey in which there is no end or final arrival.

This book will help guide you in your daily approaches to becoming a better advocate in education. For more than a decade, I've interacted with many educators who have asked questions about what language they can use to address their concerns. See, for some of us, doing this work may mean that we might have to place our professional relationships at risk. It might even cause us to jeopardize our jobs and positions in our school's community.

I get it; it's not always fun to tell peers that what they said or did negatively impacts a particular group of people.

We live in a world where being nice is often the preferred approach to communication. Unfortunately, racism, discrimination, and bigotry exist. My thoughts are, *Should we be so concerned about being nice and about other people's feelings when they didn't consider a nice approach to us or others when they said what they said?* For example, in some areas of the United States such as the Midwest and the South, being nice is a cultural standard. Calling someone out goes against the unwritten protocols in communication, but being nice doesn't always equate to change. Compromising our beliefs regarding what is right and what is wrong does not equate to change. However, I hear you, and I want to help. My goal is to provide multiple ways for you to interact with others to teach you strategies to address injustices tactfully. Some of us are bolder than others and have more experience dealing with implicit and explicit instances that negatively impact our schools. Some of us are brand new to the concept of equity and want to learn how we can develop our advocacy skills. Finally, some of us are in leadership positions and have a more significant impact on leading change. However, creating staff buy-in is a challenge. No matter where you are in your journey toward equity, I'm here to increase your knowledge and confidence in this work. However, before we get started, let's talk about the word *ally*.

A common question that I get involves some form of "Sheldon, I want to do better. I want to help others and be an ally. I want to be a voice and support my peers, colleagues, students, and parents. Nonetheless, situations occur, and I don't necessarily know the terminology. What should I say?" I like to give educators the tools and resources necessary to ensure equity at their school. I try to give the language they need and provide them with examples of situations by saying, "This is what I said. This is what I would say in these types of situations," to help folks out. As I started thinking about many of my experiences as an educator and as an individual doing this work, I started thinking about that word, *ally*.

I'm No Longer an Ally, and Here's Why

I remember doing my student teaching. I'm not going to tell you how long ago it was, but it was a while ago. Let's say that. I was a young lad. I remember going to one of the schools, and I recall being in a teachers' lounge and just kind of listening to some of the teachers as they talked about the school and some of the students. I'll be honest. I didn't feel very comfortable with how some of the teachers were talking about the students. "This is a brand-new environment; who am I?" I thought to myself, *I'm just a student-teacher. I don't have any clout.*

I listened to some of the staff members make some negative comments about some of the students who were labeled as troublemakers or students who weren't seen favorably by some of the other staff members. I remember not saying anything. I just figured, *You know what. I'm new here, and even though I don't like what I'm hearing, I'm just going to walk away and not engage in this conversation.* I left the staff lounge, and I don't think I went back there throughout the rest of my student teaching.

I shared this story with one of the professors at my university. I used to love talking to this woman because she was one of those individuals who spoke her mind, and she didn't hold back. As I'm sharing this story, I'm smiling. I was like, *I walked away because I didn't want any part in this conversation.* I'll never forget what she said to me. She said these five words, "And what did you do?" See, when I was at that school and I was developing my teaching skills, I thought I was doing the right thing by just walking away and not engaging in the conversation. I had been student teaching at the school long enough to know who they were discussing, but I was a student teacher. I wasn't even certified. It was my last year in college. I was brand new. No one knew who I was. Who was I? I thought the right thing was just to walk away and not say anything.

Not Doing Anything Is Not Doing Anything

I saw the disappointment in her face because I responded, "Well, I didn't do anything. I left." At that moment, I came to the realization that not doing anything was not doing anything. Does that make sense? Not doing anything was not doing anything at all. Let me interject. Sometimes, we have opportunities when we overhear something or witness something. We may be in a staff meeting, and the things that are being said and discussed make us feel like we should raise our hand and speak up. We may think, *Let me stop this.* However, sometimes, our positionality and confidence may hinder us. I feel like the phrase *imposter syndrome* gets thrown round a lot. We start to wonder, *Who am I to be in this space?*

I'll never forget those five words the professor said to me, "And what did you do?" Those words had me thinking, *Oh man, I didn't do anything. I thought I did the right thing by not responding and just walking away.* What I realized is I could have said something. I could have said something such as, "You know what? I know I'm new here. I know I'm not even staff, but I must be honest. I'm a little disappointed because I'm really excited about being an educator. I'm a candidate right now, and it's kind of disappointing to hear the negativity being spoken to our students." I could have left it there. I could have gone even further and said, "I haven't been here long, and I don't know the student's back story. However, he's a human being, and I think he deserves a chance. If we take the time to create that relationship, maybe we wouldn't feel that way."

The thing about the term *ally*, to be honest, is that allyship isn't precisely what's needed right now at this moment. Furthermore, allyship can become very performative. Sometimes I hear the question, "Will things change when it comes to equality or when it comes to folks being treated fairly or the end of racism? Will that happen in our lifetime? Or will these things continue from generation to generation to generation to generation?" I think the reason things continue to be the way they are, especially for those who want to end things, is that we never say or do anything to change the way we think about others. It is ineffective to say, "Yes, what's happening is wrong," but we don't do anything about it. If we just say, "I wish that things were different, but I want to be a safe space, so therefore, I'm an ally" or "I have a poster, and I have a sign or BLM flag in my classroom" or things like that, where's the action?

Unfortunately, a lot of the allyship can become performative very quickly. Now, you might have heard the term *performative wokeness*, but what does it mean? According to Lizzy Bowes (2017), "Performative wokeness is a superficial show of solidarity with minority and oppressed bodies of people that enables people to reap the social benefits of 'wokeness' without actually undertaking any of the necessary legwork to combat injustice and inequality." I like this definition because at the end of the day, the question that I have for you is, "Well, what are your motives?"

Yes, we're educators. We want to be there for our kids. We want to support them, and I think we can all agree that no matter what your views are, we want the best for our students. John Dewey said, "What the best and wisest parent wants for his child, that must we want for all the children of the community. Anything less is unlovely and, left unchecked, destroys our democracy." I think we can agree that we want the best for our students as if they are our own flesh and blood, but what are your motives?

What Are Your Motives?

I did a training with a group of teacher candidates a while ago. A good professor colleague of mine invited me to lead the training, and he asked me talk about equity in education. After providing my lecture, I opened the floor for some Q&A. I love to do Q&A because when I prepare a lesson for some group with whom I'm going to work, I assume that I'm delivering information and engagement based off what is needed. I love to follow up with Q&A because maybe I missed something or maybe I didn't touch on a question or a topic that an individual in the audience might have had.

A young white woman raised her hand. She said, "I am finishing up my teacher program soon, and I am very into equity work. I want to be the best teacher I can be and be there for my students. Should I go to an urban school, or should I go to a suburban school?" I remember responding with, "I can't answer that question. What are your motives? I don't know you. I know nothing about you. I don't know if you are saying, 'I feel like I can do good at an urban school, teach kids, and help provide a voice and advocacy work. Should I go to a suburban school, provide a voice, and teach our students in those schools about social justice.'" I went on to say, "The bottom line is, be your authentic self. Kids can tell when someone is putting on a show. Kids can tell when someone's motives aren't genuine. Just because you're an educator does not mean that your students, parents, guardians, and community know that you have the best intentions. You can say that in your opening welcome letter. You can say that in your weekly newsletters, but are you showing that through your actions? Whether you decide to work in a school that's primarily Black and Brown or at a primarily white school, I think at the end of the day, we're doing our kids a disservice if our intentions aren't genuine. Are you coming to a school because you feel like you need to save that community?

Are you coming to the school because it's just another paycheck for you? Are you coming because you recognize that for our educational system to change and for us to develop future good citizens, we must respect each other and respect our different opinions? We must learn to help others. We need you to be there to support students in that manner and teach them those other life skills and prepare them for life outside your classroom."

I don't believe in the phrase "preparing students for the real world" because school is the real world as well. However, preparing them with the skills they need to operate as adults is not indoctrination. It's just teaching your kids to be good people and good human beings. What are your motives?

Unfortunately, I sometimes get to the place of trying to figure out what's next. We live in a world, especially if you're in the United States, where the media dictates a lot of our beliefs. I have a newscaster friend who once told me the way the media selects stories. The mantra was, "If it bleeds, it leads." It often takes a tragedy for folks to start to listen. We support various causes for whatever reason, but I always wonder sometimes if there is more that I can do as Sheldon Eakins? Did I do enough? Can I do more? Are there topics on my podcast that I haven't covered that I need to cover? Are there topics that I should cover more? I question myself a lot because as I say on my Leading Equity Podcast every time, "Welcome advocates." I talk about being an advocate. I say it in my newsletters. I talk about advocacy, but sometimes I wonder, am I doing enough?

I believe that if I were to say that I'm an ally, I feel like that's a self-proclaimed title. I don't know a lot of people who call each other allies; maybe it's my circles that I hang around, but I don't know a lot of people who say, "Oh yeah, that individual is an ally." I hear many people say that they are an ally to someone else. They give themselves that title, but if I were to ask one of their students or if I asked a parent who knows them or a colleague who knows them, what would their response be? Would they say, "Yeah, I believe that this person is an ally." Then, I guess it also depends on the answer to the question, "Is that person okay with just being a safe space?" My good friend, Ken Shelton, always says, "Safe for who?"

Becoming a Disruptor

Years ago, I lived in Oregon, and I joined the NAACP because I wanted to join a national organization. I figured I wanted to be a part of the movement. I have absolutely nothing against the NAACP, but my experience in this national organization made me really think, *Is there more that I could do if I'm not affiliated with a group or an organization?* I signed up to be a member and started attending the meetings. We would talk about various initiatives that we were working on. One meeting, I looked at the chapter president, thinking, *He seems a little frustrated.* It seemed like sometimes he was hitting walls. He would say, "Okay, I just met with this individual" or "I met with this organization" or "I met with the city's this or that, but it still didn't produce the outcomes that we were hoping for." Sometimes, it seemed like the doors would get closed in our faces.

We were advocating, organizing, and talking about different initiatives that we would love to see changed. A lot of the stuff was simple stuff. It wasn't even a big deal like passing new laws or mandates. Some of it was just simple strategies such as getting some new books at a school that could utilize books but didn't have the funding. (Crickets.) Some of it wasn't the biggest ask if that makes sense. You may not be aware that this is happening, but it seemed like sometimes (a lot of times rather) folks just didn't want to hear what we had to say. I believe the defense mechanisms for many folks in positions of power would be triggered when we would approach them with our concerns. Could it have been because we were affiliated with a national organization dedicated to civil rights and equality?

During my time as a member of the NAACP, a white supremacist named Dylann Roof went into a church and killed Clementa C. Pinckney, Cynthia Graham Hurd, Susie Jackson, Ethel Lee Lance, Depayne Middleton-Doctor, Tywanza Sanders, Daniel L. Simmons, Sharonda Coleman-Singleton, and Myra Thompson. Nine innocent church members were worshipping. All of the sudden, our phones started ringing off the hook. "Can the NAACP come speak? Can you participate in this vigil? Can you do this? Can you do that?" I started thinking, *Man where were you before this?* It seemed like sometimes we were hitting walls, and then suddenly, tragedy happened, and people wanted to listen. They said, "Now, we want to hear what you have to say, but we want to hear what you have to say regarding this recent tragedy." I hate that it takes tragedy sometimes for folks to want to listen. Even when they want to listen, often they want to listen to only what they want to hear. They say, "Just make your statement about what happened. We don't have a statement of our own, so we will just use what you say and second it."

There's that level of comfort. I get it. Conversations at any level regarding race may be difficult for some of us. Again, I appreciate my time as a member of the NAACP; I just started to think that I might be able to do more as an individual versus my affiliation with a recognized entity. Sometimes, when people see those national organizations and people know what they represent, some folks automatically will start to get defensive, or they automatically think or assume that you have an agenda because you're with that group as opposed to me being Sheldon and advocating as a member of the community.

When you look at the definitions of *ally* and *disruptor*, according to Merriam-Webster, the definition for ally is "to join yourself with another person, group, et cetera, in order to get or give support." See, nowhere does it say anything about actionable steps in that definition. I can get or give support, but how does that look? I prefer the term *disruptor*. You might hear people say *co-conspirator*, and I think advocacy and activism can be put in there as well. However, I like the term *disruptor*, because the definition of a disruptor is "to break apart; to interrupt the normal course or unity of; to break apart." An advocate is a person who recognizes that we do live in an unjust society. Advocates are not satisfied with the status quo, and they're willing to speak up on behalf of others.

My final question to you is, "What are you?"

Acknowledgments

The idea of writing a book was a dream of mine, and the opportunity to publish this book came right at a time when I was dealing with personal challenges in my life. I could not have accomplished this goal without the support and prayers from Dr. Sawsan Jaber, Dr. LaWanda Wesley, Dr. Josue Falaise, Dr. Naima Duncan, Mr. Joe Truss, Ms. Mona Elleithee, Ms. Sandra Clough, Dr. Yolanda Sealey-Ruiz, and Mr. Alex Horton. You are all influential people in my life. Thank you for allowing me to be vulnerable with you and lifting my spirits.

To my Leading Equity Center team, Sara Price, Popsy Kanagaratnam, Darlene Reyes, and Margaret Harris-Shoates, thank you for believing in me and Leading Equity. Sara, I can't thank you enough for helping me stay organized and editing my transcripts. Popsy, you have been with me since the very beginning, and your work with the Weekend Voice is priceless. Margaret, you are one of the most creative individuals I know. Thank you for all of the resources that you have designed for me. Darlene, you have done a phenomenal job working with our student affinity groups. I know that you will continue to do great things. Without the support of the Leading Equity Center (LEC) team, this book would not have been written. Thank you all for your roles in supporting this work and easing my writing stress while maintaining the LEC.

Furthermore, I would like to thank the students and staff at the Shoshone-Bannock Jr./Sr. High School. I learned so much from my time working with you. Thank you for embracing me and making me feel like a member of your community. The generosity and fellowship humble me. I truly believe the motto "We are a small school. . .but a big family."

I would be remiss if I did not mention Ms. Jenny Magiera and the rest of the OVA family for the continued support of the Leading Equity Center. My experience in Chicago helped me develop the storytelling skills that have allowed me to confidently speak on stage and ultimately share my stories throughout this book.

I am thankful for the conversations I have had with Principal Kafele, Ken Shelton, Dee Lanier, Ron Madison, Jeff Gargas, and Jorge Valenzuela. I consider all of you as brothers and appreciate your perspectives of education that have inspired many of my thoughts for this book.

Writing is not my favorite thing, as I tend to write as I talk. It's often hard for me to translate my thoughts into readable content. That's why I always say that I podcast for a reason. I want to thank Tom Dinse for your honest feedback and editing of this book. I also thank Dr. Joel Boyce for your editing services.

To Amy Fandrei and the rest of the Jossey-Bass/Wiley team, thank you for believing in this work.

Finally, I want to thank my family. To my parents, Dr. Lewis Eakins and Ms. Denese Eakins. Thank you for your faith, prayers, and guidance. To my sister, Colleen, and my brother, Justin, thank you for being the best siblings anyone could ask for. To my two children, Laila and Sheldon Jr., thank you for never complaining when I had to write, for your patience, and for being the most amazing kids. Daddy loves you.

About the Author

Sheldon L. Eakins, PhD, is the founder of the Leading Equity Center and host of the Leading Equity Podcast. With more than a decade in education, he has served as a teacher, principal, adjunct professor, and director of special education.

Dr. Eakins has a passion for helping educators accomplish equitable practices in their schools. He has earned a BS degree in social science education, an MS degree in educational leadership, and a PhD in K-12 education.

Know Your Biases and Recognize Your Position of Privilege as an Educator

This chapter discusses how our biases and privilege may impact our decisions in an unconscious manner. I'll begin with sharing my experience of realizing how my excitement in my personal life illuminated a few of my privileges. Sometimes, when we hear the word *privilege*, we default to the popular term *white privilege*. The reality is, though, we all have some form of privilege. I will move into discussing ways that we can assess our biases and privilege, build relationships, and ultimately address others when we witness bias at school.

Dialing Things Back

I remember sharing with a group of my students about a cruise I was on a few years ago. "Oh man," I told them, "I went on a cruise with my kids during the winter break, and we had so much fun, and these are all the things that we did. I took my kids here, and we did this, and we did that. We went on this excursion." As I was talking to my students, one of them raised their hand and said, "Dr. Eakins, I've never even been on a boat." Another student said, "I've never even left the reservation." A third student said, "Well, that sounds really cool." I could see on their faces that my privilege was showing. I realized that I needed to dial it back a little bit.

It's not that I can't share an experience with a student, but rather, it's essential to recognize that some of my students haven't had or will never have similar experiences.

On the other hand, we can't avoid those conversations completely as teachers. How can we frame them? We can try to say it in a way that motivates students to think, "You know what? Maybe I should get my college degree. Maybe I should become a teacher. I'm encouraged because look, my teacher, someone I respect, has shared about some of the experiences that he had. Those are some experiences that I would like to have too. How do I get there?"

I believe that when it comes to how we approach education, we must start to recognize how our beliefs impact the decisions we make. The conversations we have in class and the content we choose to show our students often are influenced by how we view the world.

Consider where you grew up and what your family dynamics are. How diverse was the population and area where you were raised? If you can answer, "Well, I grew up in a very diverse community," my next question is, "How diverse was your social circle?" Although you may have grown up in a town that had many cultures, races, and ethnicities, that doesn't mean that you were immersed in cultures other than your own.

Assessing Your Affinity Bias

Whenever I conduct a training on bias, I like to do an activity with the audience. Let's try this! Grab a pen and paper and list at least six people you trust. These should be nonfamily members, so they can't be your brother or sister, mom, and dad. This activity is a lot better when you have more people, so if you can list more than six people, that is even better.

Your definition of trust might be, "If I give this person $5, I trust that they will give me my money back." It might be that you'd trust this person to babysit your children.

Next, put a check next to everyone who is the same race as you. Then I want you to put a check next to everyone who is the same gender as you. Ditto for religion—not denominational religion like Baptist or Lutheran or whatever, but if you're both Christian or atheist or Jewish or Hindu or Sikh or Muslim. Next, I want you to put a check next to everyone who is similar in age. Now, put a check next to everyone who shares your political views. Finally, I want you to put a check next to anyone who shares the same sexual preference as you.

Now, I want you to look at your list. Do you have a lot of checks?

Yes? Okay, guess what? My circle of trust would be the same. I would have lots and lots and lots of checks. Although I live in Idaho, I would still have a lot of checks next to those who I trust. This is called *affinity bias*. It's not necessarily a bad thing.

We typically like to hang around or interact with people who are like minded and who are similar in age, race, and gender. We typically gravitate toward that. Married people tend to hang around other married people. Married people with kids tend to hang around with married people with kids. Single folks tend to do the same. It's not a bad thing to have an affinity bias. We gravitate to or are attracted to things or people who are very similar to us. We can have a conversation with someone who shares a lot of the same political views as us or who shares the same interests that we have—that's fine. But let's consider ways to connect with people outside of our social circles.

Steps to Building Relationships

How can you develop meaningful relationships with students who don't look like you? When we can become more aware of our biases, we can start to improve upon our interactions with others, decrease our sense of discomfort in interacting with social groups different than our groups, and ultimately make better decisions. Use the following guide as a starting point for developing authentic relationships with students from diverse backgrounds.

My Students...	Try This!
...have a different ethnic or racial background than me.	Celebrate your students' rich cultural heritage. One simple way to do this is by expressing a genuine interest in their backgrounds. Invite students to incorporate their culture into the learning artifacts they produce. Another way to celebrate students' racial and ethnic backgrounds is to show your appreciation by representing individuals from those backgrounds in your classroom resources and curriculum.
...speak a different language than me.	Students who speak a language other than English as their first language are often viewed through a deficit lens. Value your students' linguistic diversity as enriching, not limiting. Try incorporating content-specific vocabulary in multiple languages into your lessons. This will position you as a learner right alongside your students!
...have different cultural norms than my norms.	Many students subscribe to a different set of cultural norms at home than the dominant norms imposed at school. Seek to understand and respect your students' cultural norms, especially in the process of creating your own classroom procedures or community agreements. Invite students to be equal partners in this process as you construct a learning environment that supports the safety and success of all.
...are much younger than me.	Individuals across generations often have shared interests— you just must discover them! Discuss your interests with your students and allow them to share their interests with you. You may be surprised by what you find! Try to make an intentional effort to incorporate your students' interests in your classroom learning activities.
...dress differently than me.	Be aware of your implicit biases and take steps to mitigate them. Focus on each student as an individual learner with unique strengths and talents. Incorporate strategies such as student interest surveys or classroom circles to get to know each student beyond the surface level.

Your Bias Is Showing

Although we may not realize it, implicit bias impacts the decisions we make as educators. I have biases; we all do. Does that make us bad people? No, I don't think so. In fact, biases are part of human nature. However, I believe it's essential that we recognize and own those biases that we have and find ways to overcome and challenge them.

The Ohio State University's Kirwin Institute, a leading research group in the field of implicit bias, defines implicit bias as the attitudes or stereotypes that affect our understanding, actions, and decisions in an unconscious manner.

Often, the biases that we have come from stereotypes, and they're implicit, meaning they're unconscious. We're not necessarily thinking about the situation; they're just revealed by things we do that may come from our backgrounds, lived experiences, and social circles. The important thing is to check yourself whenever you notice that you are acting on your biases. Take a step back and reflect. *Why was this my immediate reaction? Why did I respond this way? How could I have responded? How should I answer the next time a situation like this arises?*

Implicit Bias and Me

How do I cope with implicit bias when it happens to me? The following is an individual reflection guide that will help you unpack your personal experiences with implicit bias as both an agent of bias and a recipient of bias.

Reflect on a time you have been on the receiving end of implicit bias:

- What emotions did you feel?
- Did you choose to address the bias? Why or why not?
- How did this situation impact how you were treated by others?
- Were you satisfied with how the situation was resolved? Why or why not?
- How did this situation influence your future behaviors or beliefs?

Reflect on a time you have acted out of implicit bias toward someone else:

- What emotions did you feel during the interaction? After the interaction?
- Did you address the bias once you recognized it? Why or why not?
- What harm did this interaction cause to the individual or community? Were you able to repair it?
- How did this situation influence your future behaviors or beliefs?

Implicit Bias Analysis Guide

Let's take a moment to analyze our personal beliefs. The following is a two-part tool that will help you unpack specific behaviors to identify if those behaviors may be rooted in implicit biases. This tool consists of a list of yes/no questions and a brief reflection for each question.

Part 1	Part 2
Carefully read each statement in this column. • Circle "Yes" if the statement accurately reflects your beliefs or behaviors. • Circle "No" if the statement does not accurately reflect your beliefs or behaviors. If you have never been in the scenario described, do your best to predict how you might respond in the situation.	If you circled "Yes" for any of the statements in the left column, reflect on the ideas, perspectives, and questions outlined in the following text. Consider how your behaviors may be influenced unconsciously by specific attitudes or stereotypes.
I prefer to watch news channels that do not make a big deal about race. I would rather hear about the positive things happening in the world! Yes　　No	We know that media bias can influence our feelings toward topics covered in the news, including race. Additionally, our discomfort around race topics may engender a biased, negative perception of racial issues in the media. How does talking about or hearing about race make you feel? Anxious? Nervous? Uncomfortable? Try to isolate the factors that trigger these feelings to begin the process of identifying unconscious bias.
When someone brings up race at work, I try to change the subject. Race is an inappropriate topic to discuss in a professional environment. Yes　　No	Race is a component of identity, and identity influences how we interact with each other in a variety of settings. In your professional context, is it essential for you to understand how your co-workers experience the world? Why or why not? What is accomplished or sacrificed by avoiding discussions about race in professional settings?
If one of my friends makes an insensitive joke about race or gender, I will just ignore them if no one from that race or gender is around to be offended by it. Yes　　No	How do you gauge who should be offended by an insensitive remark? If you recognize a comment as insensitive to a particular group of people, does that comment offend you? Why or why not? What are the implications of remaining silent when you hear racist or sexist comments? What are the potential ramifications?

(Continued)

I am friends with people from different cultural backgrounds, but I do not invite them to social gatherings because I know they would not be comfortable.
Yes   No

Consider the individuals you interact with on a social level. How diverse is your social universe? What factors contribute to the cultural diversity of your friend groups? What elements of a typical social gathering do you think might prompt discomfort for individuals of a different cultural background?

If a student's name is hard to pronounce, I try to avoid saying it in front of the class so they will not be embarrassed.
Yes   No

If you publicly mispronounce a student's name, how will you feel? Embarrassed? Are you centering the student's feelings or your own? What is the consequence of refusing to say a person's name? What does this imply about the importance of his/her identity?

I try to make sure that I speak loudly and slowly when I meet people who look like they are from a different country so they will understand me better.
Yes   No

Should we assume that individuals who dress in a way that reflects a cultural or ethnic background are not American? How might our actions convey an assumption that people who speak a language other than English are somehow impaired or deficient?

I generally choose professionals who are older than me because they probably know what they're doing.
Yes   No

What assumptions might you hold about the competence of young professionals? What stereotypes about younger generations might support young people's perceptions that they are less capable, less professional, or less intelligent?

When I enter a room full of strangers, I seek out people who look like me (similar age, same gender, similar style of dress).
Yes   No

We often seek out familiarity to increase our sense of comfort or security in unfamiliar situations. Why do you think this is? Does diversity cause us discomfort? Is diversity inconvenient?

When I go to the bank, I will let people in front of me in line so I can wait for a nicer or friendly-looking teller to become available.
Yes   No

How does a nice person or a close individual look? Can a skin color look unfriendly? What about a hijab? How might your conception of a "nice" appearance have been influenced by your environment, beliefs, or upbringing?

I have ended a romantic relationship because I felt too uncomfortable with an aspect of the person's physical appearance (e.g., physical disability, skin color, weight).
Yes   No

You've likely heard the saying that opposites attract, but what differences qualify as insurmountable? Think about the differences you are willing and unwilling to accept in a romantic partner. How many unacceptable features are physical traits? What might this indicate about your unconscious biases?

When I buy gifts for children, I look up toys that are popular for little girls or little boys, depending on their gender.
Yes   No

What assumptions do we make about gender as it relates to children's interests and abilities? What harm might those assumptions potentially impose on young children?

When I notice a same-sex couple in public, I try to pretend like I don't see them. I am sure they would not appreciate being singled out.
Yes   No

When you see a same-sex couple in public, what feelings do you notice within yourself? Often, we may react to discomfort with avoidance. However, choosing to ignore individuals who are different from us is committing an erasure that ultimately can perpetuate harm and overlook injustice.

I treat all my students the same regardless of their physical characteristics or cognitive abilities. That's the fair thing to do.
Yes   No

What is the difference between equality and equity? Is it possible to meet students' individual needs without acknowledging their unique identities, backgrounds, and characteristics?

I have asked to switch seats at a restaurant or on a plane to distance myself from a person who is dressed strangely.
Yes   No

What qualifies as "strange" attire to you? What assumptions do we hold about culture or class that might inform the level of threat that we infer from a person's appearance?

If I see a person paying with coupons or food stamps at the grocery store, I will try to pick a different checkout line.
Yes   No

Taken at face value, this may seem like a decision based purely on convenience and efficiency. However, think deeply about what thoughts or emotions this situation creates for you. What assumptions about socioeconomic class might influence your decision to distance yourself from an individual using coupons or a government assistance program?

(Continued)

If I noticed a person making strange involuntary noises in public, I would call the police. That person could be a danger to themself or to someone else. Yes No	When you recognize signs of mental illness, how do you react? How does your knowledge about a particular behavior or disorder inform that reaction? What assumptions do you hold about individuals who live with mental illnesses?

Implicit Bias Talk Moves

Educators often ask me for ways to address/intervene when we witness bias taking place. Here is a list of sentence stems and conversation starters that will empower educators to discuss implicit bias with students and colleagues. While it is crucial to confront biased behavior, discrimination, and racism, these conversation stems are not intended to force conversations, but rather, they are designed to invite productive engagement between individuals.

Initiating Conversations About Implicit Bias

Use these conversation starters to proactively start a dialogue about implicit bias when there is no specific behavior or harm to be addressed.

Are you willing to have an honest dialogue with me about. . . ?

This question empowers the other person to consent or decline, based on their assessment of their readiness to engage productively.

It's important to me that we discuss. . .

This statement prioritizes the conversation as something that matters to you personally. It conveys to the other individual that if they respect you, they also should treat the discussion with respect.

Challenging Implicit Biases

Use these conversation starters after an individual has made a statement that conveys implicit bias.

I have a different perspective. May I share it with you?

This response does not indict the individual or tell the other person that they are wrong. However, it does cue the other person in that you are going to share something that may be in opposition to their beliefs. This conversation stem invites the other person to listen if they are ready or decline if they are not.

Can you tell me why you feel that way?

This response prompts the individual to dig beneath surface-level stereotypes or misconceptions and unpack the true nature of their feelings or beliefs.

Addressing Biased Behavior

Use these conversation starters after you have witnessed a person do or say something offensive.

When I saw/heard _____, I felt. . .

This statement begins with an objective observation before sharing your feelings. It does not presume that the other person acted intentionally out of malice and allows you to challenge their perspective.

Let's take a moment to consider how _____ might have felt when they saw/heard _____.

This conversation starter signals empathy, which is essential in conversations about implicit bias. It invites individuals to enrich their perspective rather than indicting them for their actions.

Telling Your Own Story

Use these conversation starters to begin sharing your own experiences with implicit bias.

In my experience, . . .

> This statement centers on your lived experience and your truth. It encourages active listening rather than debate, as individuals engage with your narrative rather than defending their ideas.

As an individual who identifies as. . .

> This statement connects you as an individual with a broader social group. It makes it less probable for the other person to classify you as an exception or not "really" a member of that social group.
>
> Next, we will look at ways to recognize our privilege.

Recognizing Your Privilege

Let's move on to privilege. Like biases, we all have some form of privilege. There are so many kinds of privilege connected to an individual, even though sometimes, we just assume that "white privilege" is the only privilege out there. For example, I am a male, so I have male privilege. I am also Christian, which results in me having Christian privilege. I'm able-bodied, and I'm heterosexual, both privileges that equate to benefits that I have in society, which I didn't necessarily earn or ask to have.

However, these privileges benefit me nonetheless, and I must reflect upon this fact and acknowledge that some people don't have the same privileges that I enjoy. Our realities will be different because of that. Therefore, we must keep in mind that there are things that we experience that maybe our colleagues and students don't share or things we must think about that maybe our colleagues and students don't have to consider.

Now, when we're thinking about conversations about race and ways to facilitate them, we must put our biases aside and acknowledge that we are coming from our own place of privilege. We must reflect on that before we have these conversations with our students because when we try to navigate discussions through our own experiences without considering the experiences of others, the talks won't be nearly as impactful.

The bottom line is that we all must acknowledge that we have those biases. We must acknowledge that we have privileges. Then, we can use those as stepping-stones to further discussions about race and ethnicity with our students.

Preparing the Ground: Self-Reflection

The journey to fostering an equitable learning environment requires you to examine your own assumptions, biases, and positioning. Start with looking into understanding your own cultural identity. Self-reflection helps establish a method of internal investigation into why you became an educator and what the values are that you have your students. After a deep reflection on your own perceived identity and assumptions, consider taking the Implicit Association Test (IAT) at https://implicit.harvard.edu/implicit/education.html. The IAT measures attitudes and beliefs that people may be unwilling or unable to report. It may be difficult, but we must be able to see what experiences contributed to our current view of the world.

Always remember that everyone's experiences are different.

Here are some questions to ask yourself:

- Who am I as an educator and as a cultural being?

- What are my assumptions, and what are my beliefs?

- How do those beliefs and assumptions impact the way I view people who are different than me or the same as me? How do those beliefs and assumptions influence the way I interact with students, families, and their communities?

If you want to create a safe and productive environment, use these reflection questions to consider how effectively your current beliefs impact equity in your school. Keep in mind that self-reflection is an ongoing learning process of self-awareness and self-identity. Identify at least one accountability partner to help you with recognizing some areas in which you can focus on your teaching methods. The knowledge that you have about yourself informs what you believe and what you do. Furthermore, your behaviors and the things you do in the classroom inform what students believe about themselves and each other.

We all have biases, and we make judgments about others. Some of the biases are racially based on stereotypes and result from a lack of understanding of groups and cultures. It's okay to have biases because they are a natural part of who we are. The key is to recognize those biases and reflect on how to overcome them to establish a learning environment in which you have high expectations for all students regardless of your perceived knowledge of their abilities and backgrounds.

Keep in mind that the information you receive about groups of people because of how they are represented or not represented in the news, media, and books influences all of us. From a teacher's perspective, that is part of the society that is inundated with generic messages about groups of people; those messages tend to be most harmful to students of color.

Again, develop self-awareness of your biases toward your students and work to overcome them. Do not view a student's abilities from a deficit lens or associate students with labels (stereotypes, socioeconomic status, gender, or race). Those terms are labels that society uses to tell you a student is incapable of meeting high standards. Instead, view your students' backgrounds, culture, and abilities as assets to help them thrive in their learning.

Mitigating Implicit Bias

Although we may not realize it, implicit bias impacts the decisions we make as educators. Here's an overview of five common forms of implicit bias. For each type of bias, there are two concrete examples of how this bias might manifest in an educational setting. For each example, there is a corresponding scenario that shows how one might mitigate implicit bias in the situation.

Type of Bias	What Does this Bias Look Like in Action?	How Might One Mitigate This Type of Bias?
Affinity Bias Affinity bias is when a person gravitates toward individuals with whom they have an affinity, such as a common interest or experience.	An administrator reviews candidates' application materials during the hiring process and gravitates toward applicants who are like them or who are like teachers with whom they have worked. A particular student reminds a teacher of their own biological child, and the teacher unconsciously gives that student preferential treatment.	The administrator selects a diverse hiring committee and intentionally brings in candidates with a range of backgrounds, ideas, and perspectives. They recognize that overcoming biases requires us to place value in diversity. The teacher makes a concentrated effort to increase social interaction with students who are different from them. As the teacher develops these connections, they discover commonalities!

(Continued)

Type of Bias	What Does this Bias Look Like in Action?	How Might One Mitigate This Type of Bias?
Confirmation Bias Confirmation bias is the tendency for an individual to interpret new evidence as confirmation of their previously existing beliefs or theories.	A teacher notices multiple disciplinary referrals in a new student's file. When the student displays hyperactivity during class, the teacher writes them up for insubordination and noncompliance.	Before taking disciplinary actions, the teacher reflects on the underlying factors that may be influencing this student's behavior. The teacher audits their classroom resources and practices to ensure that the learning environment promotes the student's success.
	Asian American students in a particular school division have traditionally outperformed their peers in math. It becomes school practice that if an Asian American student has a high overall GPA, the school counselor encourages the student to enroll in AP Calculus.	School counselors, teachers, and leaders get to know their students as individuals to advocate for them. After identifying students' interests, educators provide them with experiences and opportunities that both reflect those interests and expose them to new ideas and perspectives.
Conformity Bias Conformity bias is a bias that is formed through peer pressure.	A first-year teacher tries to support a new student who speaks Spanish as their first language by using visuals and nonverbal cues to make the content more accessible. After learning that other teachers at the school do not offer these supports to English language learners, the first-year teacher decides not to offer them to the student either.	The first-year teacher seeks to develop a group of critical friends, who may or may not be the colleagues who work in the same building or with the same students. The teacher establishes classroom procedures that allow students to provide feedback about their experiences as learners.

Type of Bias	What Does this Bias Look Like in Action?	How Might One Mitigate This Type of Bias?
	Most high school administrators in a school division have decided to speak out in support of a zero-tolerance policy. The principal of the most culturally diverse high school is interested in restorative justice but decides to support the zero-tolerance policy since it is what the other school leaders believe is best.	The administrator sets aside time in their weekly routine to reflect on their values and their alignment with their actions. The administrator captures those values succinctly in a vision statement, mission statement, or mantra that they share publicly. The leader is comfortable with being uncomfortable!
Halo Effect Bias The halo effect bias is when a person notes one positive or exceptional aspect about an individual and allows the "halo" glow of that characteristic to sway their opinions of everything else about that individual.	African American female students who have lighter skin and longer hair are called on more frequently in class and are more frequently recommended for student leadership roles. A white student consistently performs in the top tier on their academic assessments, and the teacher frequently ignores their misbehavior and the way they mistreat other students.	The teacher tracks classroom data regarding their interactions with students, such as questioning, discipline, and rewards. When possible, the teacher enlists the help of a colleague or instructional coach to help record this data. The teacher implements regular community circles to check in with students and build a classroom community of learners based on trust and mutual respect. The teacher uses restorative practices to support students in repairing harm to each other and the community.

(Continued)

Type of Bias	What Does this Bias Look Like in Action?	How Might One Mitigate This Type of Bias?
Horn Effect Bias The horn effect is the opposite of the halo effect bias. The horn effect bias is when a person notes one negative aspect of an individual and allows that aspect to influence their perceptions of the individual's overall attributes.	A Hispanic student performs poorly on their initial assessment, and for the rest of the year, the teacher scores the student's work lower than that of their equal ability peers.	The teacher incorporates a range of assessment techniques throughout the year, which allow students' unique gifts to shine. When grading traditional assessments, the teacher practices blind grading to avoid implicit bias.
	An African American male student made a poor behavioral choice in the previous academic year, which resulted in a suspension. This year, teachers overlook his leadership capabilities and creativity, which causes him to miss out on scholarship opportunities.	Teachers at the school research and acknowledge the statistics regarding the school-to-prison pipeline. They promote programs and activities that support the social and academic success of historically marginalized students.

Reflecting on Implicit Bias: A Weeklong Journaling Exercise

Before we wrap up this chapter, I want to share with you a journal exercise that you can do to understand where your biases may originate. Follow this series of daily journal prompts to reflect honestly and individually about your personal experiences and the way they have shaped your implicit biases. At the end of the week, use your reflections to consider how your formative experiences have impacted your relationship with and development of implicit bias.

Day 1: Who Am I?

- What is your identity? How do you see yourself?
- How are you identified? How do other people see you?
- Think about the various social groups to which you belong. What do you view as your defining characteristics? What might others view as your defining characteristics?

Day 2: What Do I Value?

- Identify the five people you would consider to be the closest to you during your lifetime.
- What characteristics do these individuals have in common? Consider race, gender, age, ability, sexuality, appearance, and behaviors.
- Based on these commonalities, what can you infer about your own preferences and values?

Day 3: How Diverse Was Your Universe?

- Reflect on your interactions as a young person. What level of diversity did you encounter in your everyday experiences?
- Think about people in your outer circle (your doctor, community leaders, local business owners, etc.) versus people in your inner circle (caregivers, close friends, coaches, etc.).
- Are the two circles equally diverse?

Day 4: At First, I Thought. . . But Now I Think. . .

- What explicit principles were you taught as a child? Think about lessons or beliefs that were reinforced verbally by your parents or other significant individuals in your life.
- What values were you taught tacitly? Think about lessons or beliefs that were reinforced by habits, patterns, or ways of being.
- What role have these beliefs and principles played in your life?

Day 5: Mirrors and Windows

- Think back to your favorite TV shows, movies, songs, and books as a child. Who do they celebrate?
- Did you see yourself in them, or did they allow you to see into a world different from your own?
- Who were your role models? Why did you look up to these individuals?

Day 6: Getting Schooled

- What was your educational experience?
- What do you remember about the demographics of your school? To what social groups did your classmates belong? Did your teachers belong to those same groups?
- What do you remember about the roles and treatment of different groups of individuals in school?

> ## Day 7: Acknowledging My Biases
>
> - Reflect on how your experiences have shaped your implicit biases.
> - As an adult, what role do the experiences on which you have reflected this week play in your life?
> - How might they impact your work as an educator?

Conclusion

When we can become more aware of our biases, we can start to improve upon our interactions with others. We can decrease our sense of discomfort, interact with social groups different than our traditional groups, and ultimately make better decisions. Moreover, I know, as a person of color, it's easy for me to say this because I'm used to being the minority in just about every setting in which I participate. I mean, I live in Idaho. However, if you're a white educator addressing issues of racial implicit bias and prejudice, it may be a little difficult because of your fear of being accused of being racist.

Understand that we all have biases and being racially biased does not make you racist. It simply could be a matter of unfamiliarity with groups outside your day-to-day social settings no matter what racial or ethnic background with which you identify. I challenge you to develop authentic relationships with individuals who are different than you. Yes, it's important for your students to see you take more interest in their backgrounds, but also the relationships that we've formed outside the classroom can have an impact on implicit bias. Developing relationships with individuals outside your social and group circle may help decrease your prejudices and alter your view of negative stereotypes. Additionally, getting to know other cultures, especially the cultures of your school's community, helps you become more receptive to the diverse students in your classroom.

Get to Know Your Students

The beginning of a new school year is often stressful including setting up your classroom, maybe learning a new curriculum, discovering new school handbook policies, and welcoming a new group of students to your classroom. You may have mixed feelings at this point. Summer is over, and it seemed to go by quickly, but you are excited for a fresh start to the new school year.

What are some of the first things you do to get to know your students? How do you learn who they are and what their needs are? This chapter discusses ways to get to know students' names, personalities, and cultural backgrounds to enhance your relationship development with your students.

Let's Start with Names

Getting to know your students includes learning how to say their names. Knowing and using a student's name during and outside class recognizes that a student exists and is important. It's one thing to know who your students are when you are taking roll or grading an assignment. When are you able to pronounce a name that is not as familiar to you? Properly saying a student's name sends some important messages to a student:

- I value YOU, I accept YOU for who you are, and YOUR identity matters to me.
- Sending these messages is a large piece of cultivating a learning environment that is equitable for all students.

Think back to your days as a student in K-12 education. Who were some of the most memorable teachers that you had? I would imagine those teachers who made the most impact in your life knew your name and made a personal connection with you.

It's easy for us to pronounce names like David, Mary, or Kimberly. The same effort that it takes to pronounce what we believe to be more common names should be taken when trying to pronounce names that may be unique or culturally and/or ethnically based.

One of my core beliefs is that it is essential to pronounce a student's name the way their mother intended. My belief is that properly pronouncing something as simple as names that I find difficult to say, even if I am the only educator in the building who can say it or who takes the time to practice saying it, will make a positive impact on my student. I will honor a student who requests to use a nickname, but I will still learn their first name.

Additional Strategies That Work for Me

The following is a list of strategies I use that work for me:

- I like to tell my students "Your name is important to me. It might take some time and practice, but I will continue to try to get it right."

- A principal, teacher, or counselor who doesn't take the time to learn their students' names may appear disinterested and unapproachable. It also perpetuates discrimination. If I have 30 students in my class and I can only pronounce 25 out of the 30 students' names, what message am I sending to the other 5 students? What if those five students were youth of color or emerging multilingual students? Students who already feel marginalized in their school will continue to feel less important because the idea of pronouncing their name is considered too hard for the teachers and staff at their school.

- Let me put it another way: what if your child was one of those 5 students? How would you feel as a parent?

- Names have meaning. If you have children, I assume you went through a process of choosing your child's name. There is a certain significance that comes with naming a child, and it doesn't matter the country of origin of the name. There is usually some sort of meaning behind it.

- Please don't make comments to your students or colleagues that a student's name sounds weird or is so "unique." Instead, let students know that you really like and appreciate their names by not trying to "Americanize" their names because it is easier for you and the rest of the class.

The Power of Names

Let's start with the power of names. Why are names so important? I mean, you were given a name. I was given a name. If you have children, you've given them names. We gave or were given names for a specific reason. I want to share a story with you to set the tone, and we'll talk about it afterward.

I have a colleague named Miguel. Miguel and I used to work together for a college awareness program at the local university. One evening, Miguel called me up to talk about his day. He was upset about something that had happened to him earlier that morning. Miguel and another colleague were invited to present the college program to a group of eighth graders at a middle school. Miguel and his colleague, Linda, were in this classroom together as guests. The teacher of the class was Linda's son.

As the teacher introduced Miguel and Linda, the teacher said, "Everyone, this is Michael." Miguel paused for a second and then said, "Excuse me. No, actually, my name is Miguel, not Michael." The teacher responded with the statement, "This is America. Your name is Michael." Now, Miguel is a person of color. He's of Mexican descent, and he's experienced different forms of racism. He's experienced challenges in life such as oppression and discrimination. He's experienced that a lot. At that moment, he was shocked because sometimes racism just catches you off guard. You're not ready for it. This teacher was telling him, "No, your name is Michael because this is America. I'm not calling you Miguel. That's not what we do here."

Miguel thought to himself, *Well, I have a few options. I could press this, and I can correct this man who clearly is being disrespectful toward me, or I could choose to give my presentation, ignore him, and keep going.* The other thing about it is Linda, who is his partner and his colleague, is the mother of the teacher. Linda stepped in and said, "Son, that's not right. His name is Miguel, not Michael." However, the teacher still insisted, "No, it's Michael. This is America." Miguel decided that based on the situation, it was in his best interest to proceed with his presentation because he knew the class would benefit from what he and Linda had to share.

Miguel shared with me later that day his experience. He called me up and said, "Sheldon, this is what happened." I listened to Miguel as he fought back tears recounting his experience that day. He said, "I feel bad because that classroom was primarily Brown students, and there were a lot of students of Mexican descent. And I felt so small, so little, because I didn't stand up for myself. What do you think?" I said, "We can't beat ourselves up about situations like these. We can learn from these experiences." I also said, "You had an opportunity to stand up for yourself. You're telling students about the importance of going to college.

You're telling them why they should go to college. You have a group of students who look at you as a person with a college degree who's working on your master's degree. Moreover, you look like them. You're a role model. These eighth graders were watching how you would respond to someone disrespecting you in front the class." I reminded Miguel that he will continue to do great things and the work that he is doing is changing thousands of kids' lives who are just like how he was growing up. He was introducing students to the idea of college and living proof that it was possible. I said, "Miguel, this may not be the last time that someone insists on calling you Michael; how will you respond?"

How often do we do this to our students? Do we call our Miguels "Michael"? Do we call our Juans "John"? Do we call our Marias "Mary"? Do we call other ethnic-sounding names something like an Americanized name because it's easy for us? Imagine how students feel when this is their experience every day. Their mom or their dad chose to name them something that was meaningful for their culture, for their ethnicity, for their race or gender, or for their traditions. They go through their elementary, middle, or high school experiences with some sort of name that is not their birth name. It's not the name that their mom or their dad calls them. Their ability to perform academically can be impacted just from that. Students benefit when they have that one teacher, a handful of teachers, or even a classmate who takes the time to practice their name.

I think the same rules can apply to those students who want to be called something other than their legal name because they identify as a different gender and they want to be referenced by the correct pronouns. Part of connecting with our students is simple. It is like basic Relationships 101. What do the students want to be called? They may say, "You know what? I just like to be called whatever nickname. That's okay with me." That's fine. If you have students who identify with different genders and you want to use the correct pronouns, it may take some time. However, it can be something that you're going to focus on. Next, we will look at some strategies for learning students' names.

Strategies for Learning Students' Names

Imagine how a student might feel when a teacher does not try to pronounce their name correctly. Learning your students' names is a sign to them that they matter to you. Here are some useful tips to help with learning and pronouncing students' names. Try different techniques until you find the ones that work best for you!

Here are some useful tips to help with learning and pronouncing students' names:

- **Roster practice**—Read through your class roster several times before the first day of class so the names sound familiar when you meet your students in person. If there is a name that you are not sure how to pronounce, try to find someone who may have had the student before and ask them to help you. It is also a good practice to make a home visit or introductory call prior to school to share with your students' parents about who you are and what they should expect in your class. This is another chance to learn the phonetics of your students' names.

- **Seating charts**—If you would like to create a seating chart, leave room on the chart to write nicknames and phonetic descriptions of your students' names. You may also find attaching pictures to the names on the chart helpful.

- **Incorporate a visual approach**—During the first few days of school, you may benefit from making name tents that you can place on students' desks. Again, you may find it helpful to write names down phonetically to help with pronunciation. You also may find this helpful for both you and the students.

- **Student introduction**—Have students introduce themselves one by one. Each time students get ready to introduce themselves, they must repeat the names of the students who went before them. Keep in mind that there will be students who will only have to repeat a few students names versus a student at the end who will have to repeat everyone's name. You may want to go back to some of the earlier students and see if they can repeat the entire class roster as well. This activity is helpful for both the teacher and students. Another variation of this activity is to play two truths and a lie. This is one of my favorite icebreaker games. Basically, you must tell three things about yourself. Two of the things should be true, and one thing should be a lie. The class must guess which one is a lie.

- **Student interview**—Pair students up and have them introduce themselves using some questions about their interests (hobbies, career goals, favorite music). After a few minutes, have the students introduce their partners to the class. This is another great way to help the teacher and students learn about each other and build a classroom community.

- **Ask when needed**—Let students know that you are practicing and trying, and you will get it down.

- **Word association**—Use classic word association.

- **Inventory survey**—Creating a well-designed student interest survey may provide some valuable information about your students. Have students complete a short survey about their interests and instructional needs. You may find collecting this information helpful when you are seeking an understanding of students' needs. It also may help with mitigating implicit bias as your assumptions and prejudgments can be met with actual information directly from your students.

- **Say the name often**—Probably the most important concept on this list is repetition. Greet your students by name whenever you see them (when they are in the hallway, when they are entering your classroom, and even when you are handing back their assignments).

- **Cultural backgrounds**—Another way to learn about your students is by investigating their cultural backgrounds.

Let's move into learning ways we can integrate storytelling.

Cultural Storytelling in Action

Each of us has a story. As our classrooms are becoming more and more diverse, it is crucial for students to share their stories and their cultures to make learning relevant and authentic.

- **Integrate cultural storytelling in both monocultural and multicultural settings**—To grow as individuals and as learners, we need to hear various perspectives on ideas and engage with people who are different from us. If student learning occurs only within the silo of a monocultural environment, we run the risk of limiting students' exposure to culturally diverse populations because they are only exposed to secondhand media sources that might propagate harmful stereotypes.

- **Acknowledge families as one of the greatest resources for cultural storytelling**—For students of certain cultural backgrounds, the stories that are taught in school and the stories that are taught at home are sometimes diametrically opposed. Keep in mind that family experiences are some of the most powerful and authentic resources that we can leverage as a learning community. Invite families into the classroom to share their stories and enrich the curriculum with their experiences.

- **Connect with other classrooms and teachers**—In the age of social media, it is now easier than ever to connect with classrooms from different cultures around the world. Platforms such as Twitter, Voxer, and Facebook will allow you to find other educators interested in using cultural storytelling in their classrooms. As you seek to connect with a community of learners, stay focused on the goal of empowering students to become global citizens. Ensure that there is mutual respect between the two classrooms so students can learn with and from one another in an equal exchange.

- **Build relationships with your students**—Developing relationships is the key to unlock the power of cultural storytelling. Nurturing these relationships will create a learning environment in which students feel safe enough to engage in the vulnerable work of sharing their culture and identity with others. Positive relationships also will empower you as an educator to make instructional decisions that enable your students to thrive based on their interests, backgrounds, and abilities.

- **Remember, you're not giving your students a voice; you're listening to their voices**—Our students are cultural beings who come to us with a unique set of experiences, values, and beliefs. As you engage in cultural storytelling in your classroom, keep in mind that your role is not to give your students a voice other than the one they already have. Rather, the work is to listen to their voices, amplify their stories, and encourage them to amplify the voices of others in their communities. Next, let's discuss how we can integrate technology into our cultural storytelling.

Tech Tools for Cultural Storytelling

Each of us has a story. As our classrooms are becoming more and more diverse, it is crucial for students to share their stories and their cultures to make learning relevant and authentic. The following is a list of educational technology tools and strategies that you can use to leverage cultural storytelling in your classroom.

Before using any website or application with students, be sure to consult your school system's acceptable use policy as well as the age restrictions and privacy guidelines for the technology tool.

Flipgrid

What is it? Flipgrid is a free social learning site that leverages the power of video to amplify every student's voice and empower global citizens.

How can my students share their stories? Flipgrid has a feature called #GridPals, which enables you to connect with other educators and classrooms around the world. Students can record brief videos and respond to the videos created by other students.

Adobe Creative Cloud Express

What is it? Adobe Creative Cloud Express is a web-based design application that allows students to create professional-quality graphics, videos, and web pages easily that they can share with the world.

How can my students share their stories? Students can use video creation tools in Adobe Creative Cloud Express to design engaging multimedia stories by combining text, photos, narration, music, and more!

Book Creator

What is it? Book Creator is an online platform in which students can apply their creativity to publish digital books.

How can my students share their stories? Students can combine text, images, audio, and video to create interactive stories, personal narratives, poetry books, and other products. Individual student eBooks can also be combined easily into a single classroom publication.

Social Media

What is it? Social media refers to any number of websites and apps that allow users to share content and participate in social networking. Commonly used social media platforms for educators are Twitter, Voxer, Instagram, and Facebook.

How can my students share their stories? Consider creating a hashtag for your students' cultural storytelling artifacts. Using hashtags is a common practice across social media platforms for creating conversations. They unify discussions by connecting posts from multiple users.

Blogging

What is it? Blogging is a style of online writing in which individuals can document their journeys or share their views on a particular topic. There are several free blogging platforms for students including Edublogs and WordPress.

How can my students share their stories? Blogging can provide students with a safe environment to incorporate their interests, passions, and experiences into their writing. Consider creating a classroom blog in which students can work together to build the collective narrative of your class community.

Videoconferencing

What is it? Video conferencing allows students to chat with individuals from across the world in real time. Commonly used videoconferencing platforms for education are Skype, Zoom, and Google Meet.

How can my students share their stories? Students can use videoconferencing to interview guests or connect with classrooms from different cultures. Before you use videoconferencing, consider having students work together to prepare a list of questions or a summary of the information they would like to share.

Integrating Student Interests

Teaching through a culturally diverse lens calls for teachers to craft learning experiences that preserve students' individuality within their classrooms. The following chart offers practical ways to celebrate students' individuality by incorporating the information collected from student interest survey data. The left column presents examples of the types of topics and questions that may appear on a student interest survey. The right column suggests a method of incorporating this information into the teaching and learning process.

Student Survey Topic	Incorporation into Teaching and Learning
Student Interests Example: "If you had the chance to interview one significant person from the present and one from the past, who would you interview? What would you talk to them about?"	Use student interests to **select texts** or **generate examples** related to your unit of study. Although the content of the curriculum is generally prescribed, the topics that students choose to explore to learn the content or attain the skills often is not!
Student Pastimes Example: "What are three things you like to do when you have free time?"	As students master academic knowledge and skills, allow them to **apply this learning to their hobbies** and pastimes. For example, you might invite students to use persuasive writing skills to make a case for the greatest athlete of all time.

Student Survey Topic	Incorporation into Teaching and Learning
Student Expertise Example: "If someone came to you for information about something you know a lot about, what topic would it be?"	Leverage students' areas of expertise to **design learning groups** intentionally that bring out the best in each learner, showcase individual talents, and/or provide strategic support in targeted areas.
Students Roles Outside of the Classroom Example: "What clubs, groups, teams, or organizations do you belong to? Include both school and outside of school activities."	As you discover students' leadership and interpersonal skills outside your classroom context, use this information to **create student roles** that enhance the dynamics of your classroom or student groups.
Student Learning in Authentic Contexts Example: "Have you ever taught yourself to do something without the help of another person? If so, what?"	Remember that students are learners outside of school! Find out how your students prefer to learn when they are allowed to drive their learning. Support your students in **selecting learning strategies** that mirror how they acquire knowledge and skills in authentic contexts.
Subject-Specific Interests Example: "Rate the following *(insert subject)* topics according to your interests."	Find out what subject-specific topics your students are most interesting to your students. Use this information to **adjust your curriculum pacing** or the order of your units to promote maximum student interest and engagement.

The student survey topics and questions presented here are only a sample of the items you may choose to include on a student interest survey. As you learn more about your students' interests and identities, remember that embedding opportunities for students to make choices within the learning experiences is a simple and effective way for educators to honor diversity and celebrate individuality in the classroom.

Five-Minute Relationship Boosters

Developing relationships with your students directly impacts students' behavior in class. When students believe that you have their best interests at heart, it is easier to facilitate a culturally sustained learning environment. Use the following strategies to take five minutes of class time to make personal connections with your students.

- **Incorporate circles in your classroom**—Commonly used in restorative practices or restorative justice, classroom circles can be a great way to develop community in your classroom! Facilitating a classroom circle involves sitting with your students in a circle and sharing with them. For example, in "The Check-In Round," the teacher pitches a question to the group, and the group uses a talking stick to respond, making sure everyone gets a turn to share. For more information about how to implement circles in your classroom, see the download "Teaching Restorative Practice with Classroom Circles" at http://www.centerforrestorativeprocess.com/resources.html.

- **Schedule time for one-on-one engagement**—Use five minutes during formative assessments, such as bell work or classwork, to move throughout the classroom and stop by students' desks. While checking on a student's work, say a quick "hello" and use the moment to assess the student's demeanor. Based on this assessment, you can determine what additional support the student might need. Take this opportunity to let the students know that you care or find out what's new and exciting in their lives.

- **Find out what makes your students unique**—Every classroom is filled with various personalities. Learning about the different personalities in your classroom will help you gain a better understanding of how students will interact with each other. This will help you plan group assignments, de-escalate conflicts, and help students navigate personal challenges.

- **Make time to show students you care**—Ultimately, you must make time to show your students that you care about what is happening in their lives. Remember to make time not only for students who are having a bad day but also for the ones who are having a good day!

Bonus Strategies

Here are some bonus strategies for helping build relationships:

- **Attendance questions**—Get to know your students while you take attendance! Instead of simply calling out the names on your roster, take attendance by asking each student in the class a quick question such as: "What is the best book you've read recently? What's your weather today? If you were a candy bar, which would you be?"

- **Personalized greetings**—Show your students how much they matter as individuals by allowing each child to create a personalized handshake, high five, or call-and-response greeting to share with you when they enter class each day. Don't be afraid to let them get creative!

- **Sticky question of the day**—Place one sticky note on each student's desk as they enter the room. Then, write a question of the day on your whiteboard or chalkboard. As students enter the room, invite them to read the question and respond by writing their answer on the sticky note and putting it on the board. This is a quick and easy way to have a class conversation that includes all voices!

- **Two-by-ten**—Spend two minutes each day for ten days in a row getting to know a particular student. Make sure that you center the topic of your conversations on the student's personal interests. This can serve as a quick and easy ice-breaker, but it also will build the foundation for a positive connection and an authentic relationship.

How well do we know our students? It's not just a matter of knowing their grade levels. What do we know about them personally? In what ways have we tried to engage with our students to develop a relationship with them?

We hear a lot about the importance of relationships, and "relationships" is not a buzzword. It's not something that we say just to say it. There's a lot of weight and power when we get to know our kids on a personal level, and our students respect us. They know that we truly care about them, and that's really important. Not only is it essential that we acknowledge their identities, but also we can teach our students to embrace their differences.

Embracing Differences Activity

When we encourage students to think and talk about diversity, it helps break down barriers. As educators, we must find creative and engaging ways to facilitate classroom discussions in which students challenge each other's thinking. This student learning activity is one way to support students in engaging respectfully and learning from each other's differences.

In Preparation for the Activity: Consider the best method of pairing your students for this activity. If you are already familiar with your students, you may want to pair them thoughtfully with a partner. (If you choose to allow students to select their own partners, they still will benefit greatly from this activity!)

1. Explain to students that they will be taking a different learning route—learning from differences! Take a moment to remind students of the importance of respecting each other's experiences, beliefs, and identities. Work with your students to set appropriate discussion norms for the activity.

2. In partners, give students five minutes to generate a list of as many differences as they can identify between them. They may start with obvious differences (e.g., hair color) and progress to differences that are more difficult to discover (e.g., a favorite song).

   Option: Challenge students to come up with fifty differences within five minutes!

3. Invite each set of partners to work together to select one difference they are interested in exploring further. Encourage them to select a difference that they are comfortable discussing with each other.

4. Once partners have selected one difference to discuss, give students five minutes to generate as many questions as they can individually that are related to their partner's difference. (For example, for favorite song, these questions would work: What is your favorite line from the song? Why is it your favorite song? When is the first time you heard it? Does the song remind you of someone when you hear it? Is the song sung by your favorite artist?)

5. After each student has created their individual list, prompt partners to swap lists. Have students reflect on the list their partners have created and highlight three to five questions they are interested in discussing.

6. Invite students to engage in a dialogue about their differences and the narratives attached to them using the questions from the previous step as a guide.

Option: You may choose to provide students with conversation starters or talking stems to promote respectful dialogue.

7. Invite students to share their experiences by working together to build a collaborative narrative or co-creating an artifact that represents what they've learned about culture, individuality, or humanity.

8. Debrief with students about the benefits of diversity, the challenges of vulnerability, and the learning process.

Keep in mind that a one-time activity is not sufficient to build a culture that embraces differences. We must plan consistently and intentionally to celebrate cultural differences through teaching and learning experiences to create an environment that values the uniqueness of each student.

How Confirmation Bias Impacts Our Relationships with Students

Confirmation bias can be dangerous if we are not careful. Imagine a student, a parent, or a teacher with whom you do not get along. For whatever reason, you may question if there is something wrong with the person. A student may give you a hard time in class, and you subconsciously may look for reasons to kick the student out of your class because it's easier to manage your classroom when they are not in the room. You subconsciously may look for evidence to back up your opinions of that person. Maybe you notice that several of your students who identify with a particular group (socio-economic status, race, gender, etc.) tend to behave or perform in a certain way in your classroom. You might come to expect that behavior from them and look for it, and you may ignore behavior that doesn't conform to your expectations. Confirmation bias is pervasive in schools, and it can have a considerable impact on the decisions we make.

Confirmation bias also can lead you astray. For example, you see a parent arrive on campus. Maybe the parent has on a hoodie, gym shorts, and some flip-flops, and you say to yourself, *Oh, that parent looks like they're tough to deal with, or maybe this is that one or two times that I see the parent throughout the school year.* You believe that the parent probably is not as involved in their children's lives. You've made this judgment just based on how the parent is dressed. Maybe you ask some students, teachers, or the principal about that parent and say, "I don't know Stephen's parents, do you? What do you think about them?" You're seeking confirmation of what you suspect to be true. Maybe you'd feel different about a parent who walks in wearing a suit or a dress. You may say to yourself, *Oh, that parent looks like a very involved parent. It looks like the parent is supportive of the school.* Confirmation bias occurs when you make these assumptions and then seek confirmation of them.

I've seen confirmation bias in play with parent-teacher conferences or other school functions in which we assume a parent doesn't care about their child's education because we don't see the parent or the parent doesn't return our emails/phone calls. Subconsciously, we may seek validations that our suspicions are correct about a parent's or guardian's lack of involvement.

As teachers, when we get the roster of students in our classes, we may go to a previous teacher of our new students and ask questions. "Who's a student who was behind in reading? Who was a student who gave you a hard time with behavior?" We may go down the list and ask questions about each student. Now, I know a lot of teachers will say, "Well, I like to get a leg up and prepare for the school year, and I like to know what's going on with my students before school even starts." Here's the thing. What if you were told by your peer that Richard was a lousy student? "I couldn't get Richard to sit still. You should put his desk next to yours. Put him in the front or in the back somewhere." You may begin to prepare for a school year with Richard under the assumption that he will be a handful to deal with.

Does Richard show up to class on the very first day with his desk placed right next to your desk with a clean slate, or are you seeking confirmation that Richard is going to give you a hard time in class? Therefore, you try to be proactive instead of getting to know Richard for yourself. Because there are so many variables with student-teacher dynamics, his previous behavior might come from a completely different place than you assume. Maybe Richard and the previous teacher didn't get along for whatever reason. Perhaps Richard had a bad year. He had many personal things happening in his life that he never shared with his teacher, or his parents never shared what was going on with him with the teacher, so he acted out.

The bottom line is that kids can change, so we want to give our kids a clean slate. We want to take the time to get to know our students instead of preparing our classrooms in the light of the previous knowledge or information we have been given. Kids aren't coming in with a clean slate if we hold confirmation bias. They're not coming in with a fresh start when we have all this background knowledge that we are using against them instead of using it to help us learn about them, so we can be prepared to support them and address some of their needs

Background information on our students is not necessarily a bad thing. How we use the information is where the problems can arise. Let's take the time to get to know our students. Let's learn about them for ourselves instead of relying on previous information given to us or shared with us based on an earlier teacher's knowledge and understanding. I think that it is vital to consider.

Constructing Positive Affirmations

Due to implicit bias, we sometimes prejudge students based on their appearance or their names. Using positive affirmations with your students is one way to mitigate this bias. This classroom activity facilitation guide will walk you through a step-by-step process that you can use to construct positive affirmations with your students. This activity is best conducted near the beginning of the year or at important milestones during the year.

In Preparation for the Activity: Think about your vision for the students in your classroom. Picture your class at the end of the academic year. Who have they become? What challenges have they overcome? How have they grown as learners and as humans? Take a few minutes to journal about your vision for your class and be prepared to share it with your students when you launch the activity.

1. Introduce the activity by sharing your vision with the class. Explain that the students will be engaging in an activity that will empower them to set a vision for the class and construct a class affirmation statement. Note that an affirmation is a positive statement that you will recite regularly about who you are as a community of learners.

2. Invite students to write freely about their own vision for themselves and their classmates. Here are some guidelines you may choose to use or adapt:
   (a) Work quietly and independently for five minutes.
   (b) Don't stop writing! If you can't think of anything to write, you can begin to write "I don't know what to write."
   (c) You may write words, lyrics, pictures, doodles, etc.
   (d) Follow your thoughts wherever they take you. This writing is for you only.

3. Give students the opportunity to share aspects of their visions by engaging in a "chalk talk" discussion.
   (a) This written discussion can be facilitated using large chart paper, a whiteboard or chalkboard, or a digital collaboration space.
   (b) Give each student a marker or writing utensil.
   (c) Invite students to contribute their ideas to the collaborative space by writing them.
   (d) You also may prompt students to respond to each other's ideas in writing.

4. Have the students look at the chalk talk and infer the characteristics that are represented by their ideas.
   (a) Example: "We will stand up for ourselves and for each other." Courageous
   (b) If necessary, add these words to the chalk talk and circle them so that they stand out.

5. Have students individually to prioritize their top three to five characteristics and write them on a sticky note. Next, have each student find a partner and work together to identify their shared top three characteristics. Then, have each set of partners find another set of partners and agree on their top three characteristics as a group.

6. Give the small groups time to develop a draft of their class affirmation based on the characteristics they prioritized.
   (a) You may want to provide students with examples of positive affirmation statements.
   (b) Allow students to be creative! Their affirmations may take the form of a call and response chant, a poem, or even a song!

7. Invite students to engage in a gallery walk to provide kind, specific feedback on each group's draft.

8. Have students decide on a class affirmation by voting, combining multiple drafts, or participating in some other inclusive process.
   (a) You may want to solicit feedback from parents or families on the class affirmation.
   (b) You also may choose to share the affirmation with your building leader or other stakeholders.

9. Debrief the process with your students. Ask them, "How did this task make you feel? In what moments were you challenged? In what moments were you encouraged?"

10. Make your classroom affirmation statement visual and display it prominently in your classroom! Take time to recite it at the beginning of each day.

As you interact and develop relationships with your students, new characteristics or affirming statements may emerge. Revisit and reflect on your class affirmation statement often! Let's talk about how we can be authentic with our relationship building.

Avenues to Authenticity

Each of us has a story. As our classrooms are becoming more and more diverse, it is crucial for students to share their stories and their cultures to make learning relevant and authentic. The following resource is a strategic guide to transform standard curricular tasks into meaningful learning experiences through cultural storytelling by identifying authentic audiences and leveraging student voices.

Do Your Students' Voices Matter?

Step 1: Let's start by assessing the extent to which your current practices affirm your students' voices.

Step 2: Next, we'll look at how you can adapt your curricular tasks to leverage student voices and provide meaningful opportunities for students to share their stories with authentic audiences.

Let's pause. Take five minutes to brainstorm a list of things that you, as an educator, can do to affirm your students' voices. Here's an example to start you off. "I can invite families to attend student-led conferences."

Brainstorming Starts Now!

Now let's reflect:

- How many ideas did you identify?
- How many of these ideas are already part of your current classroom profile?
- Which of these ideas would be included in your vision of an ideal classroom?
- What are the three biggest obstacles to making your vision a reality?

We Know That Student Voices Matter, But to Whom? How Can We, As Educators, Find Authentic Audiences for Our Students' Stories?

As you plan for cultural storytelling in your classroom, you will need to analyze curricular tasks not only through the lens of equity but also through the lens of students' voices. An authentic audience may include someone to whom a student has a personal connection, a leader or expert in a particular field, or even a group of peers who can push each other's thinking. We explore these three avenues to understand how you might use cultural storytelling to create authentic learning opportunities for your students.

Audience #1: A Personal Connection   *The student shares a meaningful moment or experience with someone who has had an impact on their life.*

Here's an example of how this could look in an elementary school setting:	Think about a person who plays a positive role in your story. Write a letter to that person describing a specific time you spent with them that you never will forget.
Here's a suggested avenue to develop authenticity:	Have students send their letters to the people they wrote about either in the mail or via email. Alternatively, consider having students record videos of themselves reading the most meaningful passages from their letters and sharing those videos with the audience.

Now, ask yourself:

- What value does this authentic audience add to the original task?
- What other avenues could you use to amplify students' voices in this task?

Audience #2: An Expert Audience   *The students share innovative ideas with people of influence who can make things happen!*

Here's an example of how this could look in a middle school setting:	Who holds power in a school community? A local community? A national or global community? Choose a community to which you belong and write to the decision-makers to convince them to accept an idea for improving this community.
Here's a suggested avenue to develop authenticity:	Use videoconferencing to invite students to share their stories and ideas with individuals of influence such as local politicians, community leaders, or directors of organizations. Keep in mind that people may be more willing to connect via videoconferencing than to fly potentially across the country to visit in person!

Now, ask yourself:

• What value does this authentic audience add to the original task?

• What other avenues could you use to amplify students' voices in this task?

Audience #3: Thinking Pushers   *The students crowdsource ideas from a population of diverse perspectives, identities, and interests.*

Here's an example of how this could look in a high school setting:	Actions speak louder than words. Do you agree or disagree with this saying? First, take a position on this issue. Then, consider the arguments for the opposing position. Select and respond to one of these opposing arguments.
Here's a suggested avenue to develop authenticity:	Have students share their evidence and experience with the class by posting sticky notes around the room or facilitating an online discussion board. Encourage students to consider their peers' perspectives and stories before crafting a persuasive argument.

Now, ask yourself:

- What value does this authentic audience add to the original task?
- What other avenues could you use to amplify students' voices in this task?

Now that you've seen how you can provide meaningful opportunities for students to share their stories with authentic audiences, consider ways that you can connect cultural storytelling in the classroom.

Conclusion

Really get to know your students on a personal level. Flip back to the questions that you asked yourself at the end of Chapter 1 and transfer those questions to your students:

- Who are they students and cultural beings?
- What are their assumptions, and what are their beliefs?
- How do these beliefs and assumptions impact the way they view people who are different and the same as them, and how does this influence the way they interact with teachers, families, and their communities?

A key component to getting to know your students is trying to understand the reality of their experiences as students at the school and in their community. After you have considered these three questions, you can validate their lived experiences in your classroom.

A simple step in getting to know your students is learning your students' names and taking the time to pronounce those names instead of trying to Americanize them because it is easier and convenient. A simple gesture of practicing the pronunciation of a student's name validates to them your level of care. It shows students that they matter to you, which will open doors to help you gain the trust and respect of your students.

The bottom line is that you should love your students for who they are and not what you think they should be. Don't operate on the principle that it's okay for students to be Black and Brown but not when they are in your classroom. Don't expect them to put aside their identities in the classroom and submit to what society believes about how a student should act and what they should learn in class. Instead, ask your students questions about their interests, language, and culture to gain insight into how they are experiencing schooling.

Spend Time with Students Outside School Settings

"When a man is denied the right to live the life he believes in, he has no choice but to become an outlaw."

—*Nelson Mandela*

Have you ever listened to your students talk about what they did over the weekend or the activities in which they participated outside school? See for yourself! Intentionally visit students while they are in their community. This includes home visits, church visits, competitions, and out-of-school programs. Take the time to learn from your students in an environment outside your supervision. This helps you understand their natural behaviors and engagement with the world. Students become experts in environments in which they are comfortable to be themselves. In this chapter, I talk about how we can build relationships through connecting with students outside school environments. I'll help you explore the importance of learning about cultural norms and bringing culture into your classroom.

The Invitation

While working on the reservation, I used to love attending powwows. If you have never been to a powwow, please go if you ever get invited because it is such an amazing experience. There's so much culture, tradition, dancing, and fellowship. There's food and entertainment. It's awesome. If you have kids, take them. I love taking my kids with me; they look forward to powwows, and they get excited because it's an experience different than what they normally experience. I like to see my students dance in their traditional attire. There are different styles of dancing, and my kids watch them win awards and prizes while my students are able to be themselves.

I loved to see the attention to details that they put into their outfits. They say, "Hey, Dr. Eakins, look at what we got on." It's funny how some of the quietest kids in the class were some of the most expressive in their dance from their attire to their passion in their performance. You never would have thought that some of these students appeared to be shy in school.

I enjoyed asking my students about their performance. I wanted to talk to them about the different categories of dance and the outfits they were wearing. My students would share with me how their grandmothers made their outfits, and they would tell me about the amount of time it took for them to make their outfits. I listened to the stories behind the gathering of materials and the intricate beadwork. Yes, we did school stuff too, but it was always great to see my students light up as they shifted to being the educators/experts when they talked about the powwow. For some of us, the pressure of content delivery, standards, and accountability keeps us away from the human side of our students. Our kids are not robots. They have feelings and get excited outside the classroom as well. We can tap into those passions, and we may be able to bring that same vigor into school.

Relationship Building: Understanding Your Students' Learning Styles

Seeing your students outside the classroom may help you discover their hidden talents, their preferred language, and the practices they use to solve problems. Consider the knowledge that you gain from spending intentional time with students in their world as a blueprint to help them engage in the classroom.

Most students enjoy learning but learn better in their preferred learning style. If you are used to preparing content for your students based on your assumptions of what they need and do not need, include your students in the preparation process. You may not understand how your expectations of your students to operate in class requires them to change their natural tendencies and preferred ways to engage with content that is relevant to them. Tying in students' background initiates their creativity and exploration. Imagine how excited students would get when they have opportunities for their culture to be highlighted within the school day.

Posted prominently in the main hallway of the school on the reservation was the statement, "We're a small school but a big family." I believed that because those were not just words. As a nonindigenous staff member, I felt that I was a part of the school family. I know you might be thinking, *Oh, well you were teaching at a tribal school. It's easy to be culturally responsive in that setting.* I get it and see your perspective. Although the student population was 100 percent indigenous, the staff, including myself, was not. I learned a lot about the community I served. Many of us teach in environments in which we do not look like most of the students. We do not share similar background stories. There's a historical perspective that we may not understand. If that is the case for you, the value in participating in cultural events and activities within your school's community increases.

You might find yourself uncomfortable at first being in a space outside your classroom in which a different language is spoken, cultural practices and customs are in play, and things are happening that you don't understand. However, observing their methods of problem-solving and the way they go about doing things in their cultural world provides valuable information for you to implement in your classroom. Try to understand their world and reflect on how your classroom might look if students weren't locked into the traditional forms of what education is supposed to be (we will discuss ways to decolonize our schools in Chapter 5). Have a presence to observe and learn, and resist any urge to judge. While spending time with your students, ask yourself these questions:

- What activities bring smiles to my students' faces when they are in their natural environment?

- How would my classroom look if I incorporated the things I learned while interacting with students in their own environment?

The COVID-19 pandemic has altered the way we interact with each other and the amount of interpersonal contact we can have. I encourage safety over anything when it comes to attending events/activities. If you have these opportunities to see your students outside school in their natural environment, please do so safely.

Relationship Building: Understanding Your Students' Environmental Contexts

Let's take this conversation a step further. Relationship building with students is not limited to the classroom. I believe we can agree that smaller things such as conversations in the hallways, in the lunchroom, and during recess cultivate our relationships with students. When students respect you, they won't want to let you down. They will be willing to work hard because they know that you believe in them.

I was standing in the hallway one day outside the school resource room, and one of the staff members came up to me after the bell rang and said, "Sheldon, I watch how you interact with the students. How do you have such a good rapport with them? I'm having a little trouble with some of the kids." My response was, "I've been here nurturing relationships with this community for more than three years. You are not witnessing an overnight process. It has taken me years to get to this place, and I'm still working on strengthening many of my relationships. I always have tried to have individual connections with my students. We share many inside jokes, handshakes, and nicknames. I want my students to feel appreciated individually and not just feel as though they are just students on my roster." Patience in nurturing relationships is key.

When I first arrived on the reservation as the new director of special education, even though I had been working part-time on campus for several years through the local university, I wanted to establish my presence in my new role. I started going around to the teachers and asking them about their needs to learn how I could support them in their efforts to ensure students in our extended learning program (we didn't refer to our program as special education) received the best educational experience. I also met with my paraprofessionals to let them know that I had their back and would support them however I could.

One day within the first two weeks of my new position, I was approached by one of my staff who said that I needed to call one of our student's parents because the child was misbehaving in class. I got as much information about the situation from my staff as I could and went to the phone to call the student's mother. I never talked to the student about the situation and went straight to call the parent. I remember introducing myself to the parent and sharing what I had learned about her child's day and behavior in class. Naturally, the mom was mad at her son and asked me to put him on the phone. I did, and when he finished talking to his mom, he slammed the phone down. This was the very beginning of the school year, and that student did not speak to me for months.

We celebrated his birthday in our room, bought him a cake, invited some of his friends, and sang the birthday song to him. He thanked all the staff and friends who attended his party except for me. I did everything I could to try to connect with the student. Whenever he came to the room, I would try to work with him, but he would just ignore me or walk away.

Around April, we took all our students in the extended learning program to Six Flags. While there, I got a tap on my shoulder from the student who I felt hated my guts. As I turned around to acknowledge him, he asked, "Sheldon, wanna go on this ride with me?" Surprised, I said, "Absolutely," not knowing that he was one of those "I like to ride in the front seat of roller coasters" kind of people. As we waited in line to ride in the front of the ride, he and I talked. We joked, and we ultimately had a good time on the ride.

That student and I became close after that day. We were outside the school that day, and I believe that being in an environment that was comfortable for him made the difference. Just riding the ride with him and spending time communicating with him about life and nonschool topics allowed a door to open that I gladly went through.

Learning About Culture First

By now you should understand the benefits behind interacting with students outside the classroom. Learning about culture that is different from your own is essential to building relationships. Our classrooms look a lot different than they did 100 years ago. Today, our classes are becoming more diverse, and as our classrooms continue to look different, we need to be more attuned to cultural diversity throughout our educational systems. Unfortunately, many of our students and their languages, values, beliefs, and identities continue to be ignored. When we ignore the individuality of our students and do not allow students to see themselves within the curriculum, the hallways, and their overall experience of schooling, we are not fostering an equitable learning environment.

Instead, as educators, we need to embrace diversity and create a welcoming learning experience for all students. I'm not trying to sound cliché or make a buzzword statement. I'm making a true statement that is a long time coming. Embracing cultural diversity is dear to my heart. It's what I am most passionate about.

What Is Culture?

Whenever I facilitate training on culturally responsive teaching, I never assume that the entire audience understands culture and cultural diversity. Culture is more than an international day celebration at school or a list of holidays to acknowledge. Instead, culture is the framework from which we define ourselves as individuals. It's what makes you, you. It's what influences us and our approach to interacting with the rest of the world. It's our beliefs, what we value, and the positions or stances that we take with political matters. Therefore, we all have a culture. Often, this culture that we have intersects with multiple cultures. For example, if you are a US citizen, you may identify with American culture. I grew up in Texas, H-Town! I consider myself part of that culture, Clutch City, baby! There are other examples such as the cultures within a neighborhood or being part of the culture of the dill pickle lovers club.

Now, let's get back to our schools and our classrooms. As the demographics of our schools become increasingly diverse, we must pay attention to groups who historically have been marginalized and ignored. Fostering an equitable learning environment requires us to acknowledge and embrace the identities of our students.

We must accept our students for who they are and not spend our days forcing them to be who we want them to be based on social norms and other dominant perspectives.

What Kind of Cultural Diversity May Be Present in Your Schools?

You know they say no two snowflakes are alike. While snowflakes might appear the same, at a molecular level, it's nearly impossible for two to be the same. No two students are the same even if they share a lot of things in common. To nurture our cultural competence, we need to be willing to learn about the characteristics that our students develop that become part of their identity. Often, these characteristics or attributes are the same cultural differences that often are ignored.

Cultural Diversity Let's look at some examples of cultural differences:

- **Race**—We must recognize how skin color impacts our classrooms and not just in our classes, but our larger society. Even if we don't talk about race in our classrooms because it opens a level of discomfort for some people, race influences many decisions that are made in our schools.

- **Ethnicity**—Often used as a synonym for race, ethnicity is the culture of people often tied to a geographic area. Ethnicity may include language, heritage, religion, and customs of a group of people. Taking the time to understand the ethnic differences of your students may help you develop the cultural competency you need to meet their needs.

- **Religion**—Christianity influences many of our school policies, systems, and celebrations. How welcoming is listening to Christmas music, for example, in class or having students write letters to Santa for students who do not belong to the Christian faith or who simply do not celebrate Christmas at all?

- **Language**—Language diversity should be considered an asset in your school. A child who speaks multiple languages or a language other than English should be viewed as a strength and not as a weakness. As educators, we can't be expected to speak every language represented in our schools personally; however, we should recognize the multiple languages represented among our student body and be willing to find ways to communicate with our students and their families in their preferred language.

- **Socio-economic status (SES)**—Many of our students and their families face economic burdens that impact their ability to learn. Access to technology, attendance due to needing to take care of family burdens, or other challenges associated with financial pressures for survival may make finding time and a place to study difficult.

- **LGBTQ+**—Students who are part of the LGBTQ+ community already may be facing discrimination and prejudice in their lives because of their sexual orientation or gender identity. They shouldn't face these same discriminations and biases in their schools. Instead, our LGBTQ+ students must experience supportive and welcoming school environments in which they are physically and emotionally safe to be who they are.

I'm just scratching the surface here with some of the cultures represented in your schools. There is also the fact that many of your students will identify with multiple cultures. A child may experience school as a gay, bilingual atheist or as a Muslim immigrant.

Monoculturalism   If we ignore race, ethnicity, religion, language, SES, or LGBTQ+, we are perpetuating a monoculturalistic environment. Monoculturalism is the policy or process of supporting, advocating, or allowing the expression of the culture of a single social or ethnic group (Oxford Dictionary). We are telling our students that their identities don't matter. Even worse, in a monoculturalistic environment, students are expected to acculturate and assimilate into the norms and expectations of the dominant culture. Are we telling our students to be themselves and that we accept them for who they are, and, at the same time, are we telling them how to sit, stand, talk, and interact with others according to what we believe is the proper way? When do our youth get to be themselves? Is it only on the playground, at home, and in their neighborhood? This happens daily to many of our students. Their identities and cultures get pushed to the side, and we discipline students for not fitting the norms that were created by someone who often doesn't share the same culture or look like our students.

Fostering Cultural Awareness and Sensitivity

Sometimes, the lack of cultural awareness and cultural sensitivity stems from educators who lack an understanding or lack the interest of others outside their social in-groups. There used to be a time when both of my kids loved to play Minecraft. At first, I could care less about the game, but I did investigate it—I checked to make sure that it was appropriate for kids, and that was about it. For months, I paid little attention to the game and the conversations that my kids would have with each other about their latest build or the most recent updates that the game had. Why? It wasn't of interest to me. *It didn't impact me in any way.* Minecraft is the single best-selling video game of all time with more than 112 million monthly active players. I know this now. I know how to play the game now, and I enjoy spending time with my kids and playing the game. Now, I can only do about 20–30 minutes at a time, but guess what? I can say this now because I took the time to learn how to play the game. Can you imagine my kids' faces when I told them to teach me how to play? A 7-year-old and a 9-year-old were teaching their dad something for a change. It started with me. It started with me taking the step to learn about something that interested my children. I learned how important the game of Minecraft was to them.

I was sharing with my daughter that I had a speech to give to educators about the importance of all students feeling welcome in their schools and classrooms. I shared with her that my message was for students like her. Living in Idaho, my kids are a small percentage of students of color at their school. I asked my daughter how she feels as the only Black kid in her grade. She shared that it can be difficult at times. When she was in the third grade, she had a performance to do with the third and fourth graders at her school. She shared with me how she realized that she was the only Black kid in both third and fourth grade at her school. I told her that just like her, there are kids of other ethnicities in similar situations at their schools. Many students experience school feeling isolated and never finding the lessons relatable to them and their experiences. Everything is taught from one perspective. I told her that my message to educators is that we must ensure all students get what they need.

Imagine if every educator viewed students as if they were their own children? If you have children or a niece or nephew, you want the best for that child. However, the reality is that we are called to serve other people's children, but that doesn't mean we treat our students like other people's children.

One of my favorite movies is called *Bebe's Kids*. My favorite line from the movie is "That ain't my kids. That's Bebe's kids." The movie is about a man who is trying to impress his new girlfriend by agreeing to look after her friend Bebe's kids. He soon finds out that Bebe's kids are off the chain! He takes the kids to an amusement park, and the kids destroy the entire park. He has a terrible experience with Bebe's kids but has a change of heart when he goes to drop them off at their house and realizes that the children will be left home alone because Bebe is not there. She just left a note on the refrigerator for the man's girlfriend to feed the kids. It's hard for him to say goodbye, and he gives them his last few dollars so that they can order some dinner. He ends up going back to the apartment to spend more time with the kids despite the trouble they caused him earlier that day. He didn't go back to impress his new girlfriend. It was because he started to have empathy for Bebe's kids and their living situation.

Sadly, many educators look at students as "troublemakers" and "Bebe's kids" instead of taking the time to form relationships that allow us to see a different perspective and understand their world. Our kids start to rebel when their learning becomes frustrating or when they are forced to act and behave in ways that erase their culture. Let's look at how we can bring in the cultural experiences from our students into our classrooms.

Bringing Cultural Knowledge into Our Classrooms

Cultural diversity matters in education because students should not have to hide their identities to be successful in school. Classrooms that honor cultural diversity give students a voice, build their confidence, and alleviate the pressure to blend in with the majority. Use this resource to identify ways that you can honor students' cultural diversity by creating opportunities for them to exercise their voice and choice in their learning.

Teaching through a culturally diverse lens requires educators to weave students' culture and identities seamlessly into learning experiences. One of the simplest and most effective ways to do this is to honor students' identities by creating opportunities for them to exercise voice and choice.

- Student's voice refers to their ability to express their own ideas, beliefs, and perspectives during a learning experience.

- Student choice refers to the act of allowing them to exercise agency in making meaningful decisions about their learning journey.

Keep in mind that it may not be realistic to provide total student voice and choice within every aspect of a learning experience. Use this framework to select one or two ways that you can empower students and make culture matter.

Communication

Allow students to select from various methods of communication to convey their ideas/thinking to an audience.

Examples:

- Writing
- Speaking
- Lyrics or verse
- Asynchronous dialogue (e.g., discussion boards)
- Technology enhanced communication (e.g., speech-to-text)

Collaboration

Empower students to decide what level of collaboration best supports their work in pursuit of the learning goal.

Examples:

- Individual
- Pairs
- Small groups
- Flexible groups
- Group roles or protocols
- Community partners

Learning

Provide different avenues for students to explore to acquire curricular knowledge and skills.

Examples:

- Research
- Dialogue
- Experimentation
- Multimedia texts or resources
- Analysis of models or examples
- Fieldwork or exploration
- Hands-on tasks

Presenting

Allow students to choose a way to present their learning that showcases their unique strengths and talents.

Examples:

- Visual arts
- Performing arts
- Creative writing

- Research products (e.g., infographics)
- Simulations
- Media products (e.g., videos, podcasts)

Feedback

Consult with students to identify a feedback channel that preserves their dignity, confidence, and desire to grow.

Examples:

- One-on-one conferencing
- Written feedback (e.g., two-way journals)
- Exemplars
- Peer critique
- Self-assessment (e.g., rubric-based checklist)

Additional Ways to Become More Intentional in Embracing Culture in Our Schools

Here are additional ways to become more intentional in embracing culture in schools:

- **Develop cultural awareness**—Cultural awareness fundamentally means being aware of the multiple cultures around you. We already mentioned that culture is not just about race and ethnicity. Being culturally aware is connected to relationship building, communication, and respect because it allows you to take a step back and view the world from a different lens. Being culturally aware also may help you identify your own culture and the way it has developed you into the educator you are today.

- **Appreciate differences**—When we become culturally aware, we need to understand differences. It not always about how we can find similarities with our students.

It's okay to be different. We teach our students all the time about being different and the reasons it's okay for students to be unique. We must take on this same ideology. It's okay for us to be different from our students. It's not okay for us to demand a child become like us or that they must put aside their culture to be more like what we think a student is supposed to be—the behaviors that are acceptable or unacceptable based on our own experiences, traditions, and beliefs.

- **Remain sensitive to differences**—Keep in mind that not all students are going to be willing to discuss their culture with you and others. There are many reasons for this. A child who may be in the minority in the classroom or school already may feel isolated or unwelcome by their peers and school staff. The child may not want to be viewed as the spokesperson for their culture. There's also stereotype threat, which is when an individual is at risk of or has concerns about perpetuating a negative stereotype about their group. For example, a female-identifying student may not perform well on a math test because she believes that girls aren't as good in math as boys. A student whose first language is not English may not perform well in class because they have been treated as less intelligent than their peers.

- **Hold high expectations for all students**—We must hold high expectations for all students. Just because you embrace cultural diversity doesn't mean you should adopt diversity in your expectations. We must be consistent with maintaining high expectations for all students. Yes, you need to create an equitable learning environment by providing accommodations and differentiation for students who need it. However, we want all students to excel. If we hold multiple expectations for different students based on biases we hold toward different cultures, we are sending a message to our students that cultural differences determine our beliefs for academic outcomes.

- **Culturally sustaining pedagogy**—The reality is that the foundation of today's educational system was built and designed to educate white men. Even today, our textbooks, curriculum, and teaching force are heavily influenced from a white perspective. Therefore, as educators, we actively must cultivate a curriculum that accurately captures the world in its entirety. Women have done more than fight to earn the right to vote or sit in the front of a bus. Black people have impacted our society beyond slavery. Our indigenous communities have done more than just being the first to inhabit the land that we call America. You can change this narrative and provide a broader lens in the classroom. By doing so, you can help students who often feel marginalized know that their culture matters to you. Not only does their culture matter to you as the educator, but it must matter to their classmates and the rest of the school community.

Study what is going on in your students' community with the members within your local context. Reading books alone is not enough. Books often are written in general terms that provide an overview of being culturally responsible. Instead, remember that all communities are different, and even though there are commonalities among ethnic groups, you need to get more specific by learning from the characteristics within your students and their community. Please keep in mind that you will need to establish trust between you and your students for them to share their experiences with you.

The Trust Process

To create a learning environment in which all students can thrive, educators must earn students' trust and respect. When students believe that you have their best interests at heart, it is easier to facilitate a culturally sustained learning environment. Consider embedding the following actions into your current practice to cultivate an environment in which trust can grow:

Ensure a safe learning environment for all students.

- For students to achieve at their highest potential, they must feel safe. Building a safe learning environment in school requires that measures are put in place to ensure students' physical well-being; however, it also requires that educators attend to students' social, emotional, and academic needs.

- Consider the culture of your classroom or school building. Do students worry about teasing, bullying, or peer pressure? Are students free to be their authentic selves? When students take academic risks, are they affirmed or penalized?

- Identify potential threats to student safety and take action to minimize these threats. This may include auditing your security practices, establishing classroom norms, or adapting your own behaviors.

Take time to build community.

- When educators take time to nurture authentic relationships and build community, students are better equipped to engage as active participants in their learning. Subsequently, it makes sense for teachers and school leaders to prioritize relationships above content!

- Keep in mind that community-building activities can make a great deal of impact in a short amount of time. Consider setting aside a few minutes each day to connect with students on a personal level. For a list of relationship-building strategies that you can implement in five minutes or less, check out the resource "Five-Minute Relationship Boosters" in Chapter 2.

Be authentic.

- For students to trust you, they must have a clear understanding of who you are. Be honest with your students and be willing to share your true self. Communicate your values clearly and make sure your words and actions reflect those values.

- Honesty requires vulnerability, and vulnerability can be a difficult concept for educators to navigate with students. One powerful way to establish trust with your students is to be willing to admit when you are wrong. Own up to your mistakes and accept responsibility for your actions. This not only will demonstrate your character as an individual, but also it will set a positive example for the students in your learning community.

Build constructive partnerships with students.

- Learning should be a process in which students actively participate; however, in most cases, adults hold most of the power within the classroom. One clear indicator of a trusting learning environment is when students are valued as co-constructors of knowledge within the classroom.

- The only way for educators to establish meaningful partnerships with students is to listen to them. Promote clear, open channels of communication that students can use to provide you with regular feedback on their experiences. Be intentional about using this feedback to ensure that the learning environment is responsive to all students' needs.

Support students in making good choices.

- The best way to honor students' trust is by trusting them in return! Provide students with meaningful opportunities to make choices about their learning in ways that affirm their backgrounds, interests, and identities. This may include allowing students to study a topic of interest or empower students to choose their own learning strategy.

- Remember that making choices is a skill that must be taught, practiced, and refined. Support your students in learning to make good choices by providing scaffolds, models, and opportunities for reflection. Celebrate the diversity in your learning environment by affirming students' agency and empowering them to take control of their own learning journey.

Conclusion

It's important to remember that students don't always get to be their authentic selves at school. As a result, you may not get to see them at their best. If a student invites you to participate in an event in which they are involved, try to be there. I know we have our own busy lives, but there are so many benefits to observing students when they are passionate about their talents and cultural experiences.

Check Your Current Language Practices

This chapter talks about the importance of relationships, and part of developing relationships with our students is the way that we communicate with them. That's part of how we connect with our students. You might be asking me, "Well, what do language practices have to do with equity?" I'll start with discussing how we accept language in our classrooms according to our threshold of what we allow to be said in class. I then will discuss how you can set classroom norms, mitigate microaggressions and stereotypes, and reduce stereotype threats.

"They Robby"

I want to tell you a quick story. When I was teaching in the Virgin Islands, I was learning the language. It's funny because in the Virgin Islands, everybody speaks English, and I speak English. However, lots of words have meanings there that are different than where I'm from. These differences affected me because, as the following story illustrates, part of my process of getting to know my students was just checking in on them to hear about their weekend.

I recall a Monday morning when the kids in my classroom were unusually excited about a concert by a local artist they went to see over the weekend. I was excited with them and said, "Tell me about it. How was it?"

They were telling me about all the songs that this local artist sang, and they shared how the band played and how they felt about the experience overall. Then, they told me, "Well, after the concert, they Robby." I didn't catch their meaning at first. I said, "Excuse me?" They said, "Yeah, they Robby." I said, "Well, we were just talking about this local artist. I don't know who Robby is." They kept saying, "No, no, no, no, no. They Robby!" I said, "I'm sorry. I don't understand." Then, one of the students finally said, "Mr. Eakins, they robbed him."

I said, "Oh! My bad. My bad." I didn't understand, but again, I was connected with my students. I was taking the time to develop relationships with the kids, and I had absolutely no idea who Robby was, and I forgot that the way that they speak English was a little different than how I would speak English in the states. I'm glad one of the kids took the time and said, "No, no, no, no, no, no. They robbed him," so I could understand what they were saying because we were going back and forth for a minute.

Language

Language shapes our world because the words we use and the way we use them are tied to how we view this world. Check what your language practices are, how you are inviting students to be, and how they are expected to speak. Allow students to speak comfortably in their language.

Now, here's a question that I get from time to time regarding language. "Should students be allowed to curse in school?" I feel like this calls for a subjective answer. My short answer is, yes and no.

The first thing I want to start with is the question, "What counts as a cuss word?" Depending on who you are, what your background is, and what your lived experiences are, some words might be more acceptable than other words. Think about TV and movie ratings. This is TV-14. This is rated R. This is rated M or whatever it is. There are different ratings that are available via the television's channels and movies that you watch. You also will see it in our music. You'll see the explicit language content labels on the covers of certain albums and streaming downloads depending on the language in the lyrics. Society has said, "Okay, certain words are unacceptable, and some words are acceptable. Other words just kind of depend on how you feel." If I hear a student say, "Hell," "What the hell?" or "Damn," it may not bother me. However, if I heard the "F" word or the "S" word, my response may be different. Certain words that are acceptable to many people in everyday language may not be to you personally depending on your beliefs and background. I know many educators wouldn't want to hear any of those words, and we're not even going to get into racial slurs. We're not going to get into the insensitive and offensive "R" word (retarded) that students use to describe students with intellectual disabilities.

I have a special education background, so we're not going to bring up the "R" word or homophobic slurs because I think that's a different box. That's a different conversation. We're just talking about general curse words, not about racial slurs or slurs that impact certain groups of people. That's not what I'm talking about. I believe that if you're reading this book, you agree that those words are unacceptable. Those words are wrong, and not only do we need to shut those words down, but we also need to take the time to explain to our students why they shouldn't utilize those words.

At the end of the day, kids will test us to see where the threshold is for what they are allowed to say and do in our classroom. You might even ask, "Why do students need to curse anyway? Why do they feel that they need to utilize these words?" We say, "Oh, kids were cursing in class." Sometimes we assume that profanity occurs only in middle and high school, but that's not the case. This extends from pre-K all the way up. Yes, our little ones learn these words. Maybe they learn them at home. Maybe they learn them from TV.

When kids swear in class, in the hallways, or in school, there's often a level of acceptance by their peer group. They feel that it's cool to utilize these words. Then, there are people who express themselves this way when they're emotional. You might be saying to yourself, *What can I do about this? I will not allow any curse words in my class whatsoever.* There might be a rule in your school handbook about curse words.

The first thing to do is reflect on why some of those swear words bother you. Then, plan how to discuss with your students what words are acceptable and what are some ways they can speak to one another respectfully. I prefer not to take a negative approach and make a set of rules that say, "Don't do this." Rather, I recommend that you provide examples of the words you would love students to utilize in class. You can tell them, "This is how we speak respectfully to one another."

Notice I said "words," not "language." We're going to get to that later when I talk about setting norms. For now, I'll just say that setting these norms is helpful for your class discussions and interactions with each other, so just hang on, and I'll get there.

Now, I know that in a perfect world, you only would need to have this conversation with students one time—the first day of school. However, the likelihood is that you will need to reinforce these norms a few times. It's part of the process.

Personally, curse words don't bother me. (Again, I'm just referring to curse words.) In my career, I've interacted with cultures and communities in which, honestly, swear words are the norm. It's almost as if they aren't even considered curse words. To me, punishing students for their words and making them change their word choices is asking them to change their habits. I've witnessed situations in which students don't even recognize that they're cursing until you call them out. Sometimes, kids just forget. For a lot of them, these words are just their norm. I'm going to share a quick story with you regarding that.

A new principal comes to a school in the middle of the school year. This principal does not reflect the demographics or background of most of the student population and staff. This principal comes into the new school with their values and their beliefs, and that is how they operate and run the school.

One day the principal was in the library observing a class, and the kids were watching a video. One of the students said, "Damn. That man hit that person really hard." The principal overheard him and told the student, "Hey, you need to apologize for what you said. There are women in this room, and you need to apologize to the librarian." There are so many things wrong with that statement, but hang on. There's more.

The student refused. He said, "No, I'm not apologizing. What did I say? What did I do? All I said was, 'Damn, that man hit the person really hard.'" The principal got angry because he felt that the child was being insubordinate. He said, "If you do not apologize, I will call the police." Again, depending on your beliefs and values, that may not be a big deal. Is that worth policing? Is it worth telling a student that you will call the cops on him if he doesn't apologize? I don't think so.

The student again refused, and he became upset because he was threatened with the police. This was a student of color who had seen and interacted with the police. He didn't want to get himself in trouble or get involved in a situation, so he walked out of the library. The principal followed him and told him to stop. "You need to come to my office. You need to apologize. You're being disrespectful." The student also was saying some words, so there was a power struggle.

Now, here's a part that I want you to understand. When I talk about understanding the community that you're serving as an educator, we must keep in mind that when we are in people's community. We need to understand their culture. This principal did not. He was a by-the-book individual. He viewed education, learning, and leadership from his own understanding and background.

Here's the thing. The student's response was totally acceptable in his community and in his background. I'm not just talking about at home. His response was acceptable as a part of the community. The use of "damn" and some other words are considered curse words in some societies, but they were not curse words to him. In his community, that was how they talked. Fortunately, for the student, the other teachers who witnessed this whole scene take place were able to sit the principal down and discuss the situation with him. They let him know, "Hey, you need to understand the culture. This is acceptable language in his community."

I understand the differences between professional settings and informal settings, but this principal had to be educated about that. They told him, "Listen, you're in their space. You're serving this community. The community is not serving you, and you need to understand that what you may believe is wrong and what you may believe is not the right way is what *you* believe. Both the principal and the student apologized, and their relationship was better. I wouldn't say it's perfect, but it was better.

So Are You Saying Let Students Curse?

Now, I know what some of you might be thinking. *Well, allowing students to curse is not going to help them when they want a job or when they are in professional settings.* My advice is that students should be taught about being themselves, but they also need to learn that being themselves may come with negative consequences, if their words or actions are perceived as disrespectful. Help students learn to make choices about what they say around friends versus what they say in a professional setting. I think we need to educate kids on the benefits of expanding their vocabulary beyond those four-letter words. I want you to be open to different modes of expression and don't let communication differences become a barrier to the exchange of meaningful ideas in the classroom. I started off this chapter with the notion that we cannot forget how the way we communicate with our students impacts the relationships that we develop with them.

Here's another thing to consider. Students may feel more comfortable speaking in a mixture of their native tongue and English such as Spanglish or African American vernacular, for example. Students need to know that it is safe to engage in dialogue that is comfortable to them to spark more engagement in your classroom. For students of color, being in their comfort zone of how they can speak and how they can communicate and engage in discussions is important. It's vital. If your students talk over each other and communicate with vigor on topics that interest them, don't stifle or suppress their communication practices by structuring a rigid discussion format. Allow conversations to flow in all their complexities. Allow students to communicate freely in a familiar manner that may be uncomfortable at first because it disrupts the way we have been trained how a class discussion should operate. At first, it might feel like mayhem. However, pay attention to the richness and thought-provoking contributions that students give to class discussions.

Now, I know that this may sound difficult to do. As educators, we often want full control of our classrooms. This includes comprehending all the language used. Sometimes, things are said that we don't understand whether it's not in English or whether someone is utilizing slang. We just don't get it. Sometimes, I know it's hard to be okay with that. Listen, I challenge you to let it happen and see how the discussion develops when you participate in a student-led debate. Interruptions from students and discussions may lead to an increase of participation and engagement that may not have happened if students were called on or if the class discussions were facilitated in a manner that was deemed to be "appropriate."

Understand that not everyone engages in a calm, hand-raising, turn-taking way of discussion that is generally viewed as acceptable. That's not the only way a meaningful and intellectually rigorous discussion can unfold. Establish an atmosphere where students respect each other's opinions while you allow them to express themselves in a manner that comes naturally.

It's okay for your room to be loud if the discussions are engaging and meaningful. While loudness can be construed as unruliness, in the context of lively academic discussion, it may be indicative of a passion for and engagement with the topic. Appreciate the richness of other types of language and what the language means in learning.

If you are not allowing those kinds of conversations to unfold because they are uncomfortable for you or if you refuse to allow students to switch back and forth from their first language to a traditional English format because you don't understand everything, you are perpetuating a form of suppression that many students of color experience in school.

As the educator, if a student uses terms from another language, you are in a great position to request a translation of the term during the discussion, even if it requires an interruption. Such an overture constitutes inclusivity for both those who do understand the term and those who don't understand it. It also shows that the educators are actively engaged and interested in what the students find to be important and relevant in the discussion.

Here are some questions that I want you to ask yourself. Here's that self-reflection time.

- How am I valuing and appreciating language practices that are different from my practices?
- If I'm feeling excluded in class dialogues because I don't understand all the language being used, what can I do to engage in the conversation better?

Asking yourself these self-reflective questions places emphasis on whether your classroom norms marginalize, suppress, or hinder students' abilities to maximize learning and growth as a means of countering potentially negative outcomes.

Consider exposing yourself to new knowledge that directly ties into your students' lives. For instance, you can learn their language. This is a shift in which you are learning more about your students, but there's more to it than picking up the ability to follow conversations and knowing what students are saying when they talk in another language. You'll begin to understand what it's like to learn a second language. This will give you an appreciation of the challenges students face to articulate their thoughts that are often in a different language from their natural language.

Setting Classroom Norms for Dialogue

Sometimes, you're going to be in a situation where some conversations might be a little difficult for you to handle. When was the last time you engaged in an honest dialogue with your students about a difficult topic? You may remember how difficult that conversation was to navigate. Now, imagine facilitating a discussion about a controversial topic such as racism with an entire group of people. The difficulty intensifies.

In our current context, many educational leaders find themselves in roles where they must skillfully navigate conversations about racism and anti-racism, bias, and privilege with groups of stakeholders. I'm not a checkbox guy, but I'll give you a few guidelines for establishing conversation norms, which will enable you to facilitate challenging conversations about tough topics.

Now, why are conversation norms necessary when we're having these difficult conversations? Well, conversation norms promote equity within the discussion. Conversation norms can provide individuals with concrete strategies for communicating through strong emotions. Conversation norms can guide the discussion toward solutions and healing. Finally, conversation norms can enhance empathy and understanding.

This is a student-led discussion, so I am providing some guidelines for you to facilitate the conversations. The first guideline is to involve discussion participants in the creation of the norms. Don't just do the stuff by yourself. Conversation norms are most effective when they are produced through a collaborative process, so allow discussion participants to reflect on what they need to feel safe, respected, and valued, which may go back to what I was mentioning earlier in regard to allowing students to speak freely. Use the needs they identify as a starting point for drafting your conversation norms.

Now, the next guideline is to select a few concise norms. Consider selecting only three to five concise norms to encompass your students' needs. Keep in mind that most of the discussion participants' mental energy will be devoted to the dialogue itself. Choosing only a few conversation norms will make it easier for everyone to adhere to them as they engage in the discussion.

The next guideline is optional, but I recommend it. Display those norms prominently during the discussion to ensure that the conversation norms are clear and visible to all participants during the discussion. This will not only ensure that students can hold themselves accountable for following the norms, but also it will give them the language to interact with others if the norms need to be addressed. I want to be very clear about this. Setting up conversation norms is helpful, but don't utilize those conversation norms or rules in a manner that's going to suppress and oppress the creativity, critical thinking, and language practices of our students.

Now, here's the next guideline I would suggest. You can designate a process observer. Select an individual to keep track of the extent to which participants adhere to the norms. Explain to participants that the process observer will help the group monitor and adjust the conversation norms by noting points in a discussion when the norms are either broken or ineffective.

It's okay for your classroom to be loud. It's okay for kids to utilize their hands and be passionate in their expressions during the conversation. However, you do want to try to keep the conversation on point and relevant to the discussion's topic. Sometimes, we tend to go off track. Rather than you as the teacher being the one who's saying, "Hey, let's get back on track," we designate a process observer. That way, you're having a student support the effort of keeping the conversation on topic and keeping those norms observed.

Next, set aside time to reflect on the norms. Every participant will not adhere to every conversation norm 100 percent of the time. We talked about that. However, it's okay. Intentionally include a few minutes at the end of your allotted discussion time to allow participants to reflect individually and debrief collaboratively about the conversation norms. Invite students to acknowledge their missteps and consider the growth opportunities. Honor the participants' experience by giving them the space to engage in honest reflection.

The final step that I want you to consider is to reassess your norms often. We know that humans are complicated, and having difficult conversations is not an easy thing to do sometimes, especially when we're dealing with elementary, middle, and high school kids. Because of this, the same set of conversation norms will not work in every group or across every context. Building a community that is safe and equitable requires constant reflection and refinement. Ask students what can be done differently to promote a safer, more equitable space for dialogue in your learning environment.

These are just some conversation norms to get you started as you are seeking to create an environment where students feel safe to express themselves in whatever language is most comfortable for them.

Becoming Mindful of Microaggressions

Becoming mindful of microaggressions as an educator requires careful examination of your own behaviors and practices. Use this tool to reflect on your beliefs and actions. Carefully read each statement and select the extent to which you agree or disagree.

	Strongly Agree	Somewhat Agree	Somewhat Disagree	Strongly Disagree
1. I tend to call on my high-achieving students since they usually have the right answers. This way no one gets embarrassed.	Strongly Agree	Somewhat Agree	Somewhat Disagree	Strongly Disagree
2. I know which students I cannot trust to work in an unsupervised setting. They will get themselves into trouble if they are not constantly monitored.	Strongly Agree	Somewhat Agree	Somewhat Disagree	Strongly Disagree
3. When students are loud, they are probably off-task.	Strongly Agree	Somewhat Agree	Somewhat Disagree	Strongly Disagree
4. I think it is best to assign easier tasks and projects to lower-performing students to boost their confidence.	Strongly Agree	Somewhat Agree	Somewhat Disagree	Strongly Disagree
5. Students should have to earn the privilege of working in groups or using technology during class time by being well-behaved.	Strongly Agree	Somewhat Agree	Somewhat Disagree	Strongly Disagree

6. If a student has an IEP, that means that they require special assistance in all their academic classes.	*Strongly Agree*	*Somewhat Agree*	*Somewhat Disagree*	*Strongly Disagree*
7. It surprises me when a student with behavioral problems gets a good grade on a test or assignment.	*Strongly Agree*	*Somewhat Agree*	*Somewhat Disagree*	*Strongly Disagree*
8. If I must correct a student more than once, that means they are being defiant.	*Strongly Agree*	*Somewhat Agree*	*Somewhat Disagree*	*Strongly Disagree*
9. Every student can be successful in school if they pay attention and work hard.	*Strongly Agree*	*Somewhat Agree*	*Somewhat Disagree*	*Strongly Disagree*
10. If I teach my students to behave, they will be more successful both inside and outside school.	*Strongly Agree*	*Somewhat Agree*	*Somewhat Disagree*	*Strongly Disagree*

1. **I tend to call on my high-achieving students since they usually have the right answers. This way no one gets embarrassed.**	*Keep in mind that achievement does not always correlate to intelligence. Moreover, there is power in learning from our mistakes. Consider promoting a learning environment in which mistakes are normalized and students work together to find solutions.*
2. **I know which students I cannot trust to work in an unsupervised setting. They will get themselves into trouble if they are not constantly monitored.**	*When we develop trusting relationships with our students, it can have a significant positive impact on classroom management. Trust, however, is a two-way street! Consider to what extent your beliefs or perceptions of a student's tendency to misbehave might encourage a self-fulfilling prophecy.*

(Continued)

3. **When students are loud, they are probably off-task.**

Consider the possibility that increased volume may not equate to off-task behavior. In many cultural settings (e.g., athletic events, family gatherings, churches), loud expressions can serve as indicators of engagement or involvement. How well do you understand your students' communication styles? Do your classroom norms allow for your students to be their authentic selves as they engage in the processes of learning?

4. **I think it is best to assign easier tasks and projects to lower-performing students to boost their confidence.**

As educators, we must strive to create a learning environment in which all students feel valued. When students are aware that they are intentionally excluded from opportunities that are "above" them or are "too advanced" for them, it can cause them to feel like second-class citizens within the classroom.

5. **Students should have to earn the privilege of working in groups or using technology during class time by being well-behaved.**

Group work and technology tools are often leveraged in systems of rewards and punishment in the school setting. However, it is important to note that collaboration and technology are not rewards; they are learning strategies through which students obtain mastery of essential knowledge and skills! When we deprive students of learning opportunities based on behavior or meritocracy, we essentially are disenfranchising them.

6. **If a student has an IEP, that means that they require special assistance in all their academic classes.**

An individualized education plan or IEP is not a determination of a student's intelligence. Although students may have a specific learning disability documented in their IEP, this does not mean that they cannot achieve at high levels in academic courses. Some students may require accommodations in a particular subject that they do not need in another subject.

7. **It surprises me when a student with behavioral problems gets a good grade on a test or assignment.**

When we build a profile of a model student in our minds, we run the risk of overlooking the strengths and talents of learners who do not conform to that image. Consider setting aside time to build relationships intentionally with students who challenge you as an educator. You will likely discover the skills and abilities that will enrich the learning environment.

8. **If I must correct a student more than once, that means they are being defiant.**

Who establishes the behavioral norms in your classroom or school? Are these norms like or different from the expectations that apply in other settings in which your students exist? When we ask our students to shed their cultures or suppress their identities to fit a specific behavioral mold, we may create a dissonance that is difficult or even traumatic for a student to resolve.

9. **Every student can be successful in school if they pay attention and work hard.**

The belief that a student's success is determined by their work ethic is rooted in the myth of meritocracy. This belief fails to acknowledge any of the systemic barriers, discriminatory policies, or exclusionary practices that marginalize students within the American education system.

10. **If I teach my students to speak properly, they will be more successful both inside and outside school.**

Teaching through a culturally diverse lens requires us to embrace linguistic diversity. Touting "proper English" as the only appropriate or acceptable mode of communication pathologizes cultural expression and creates a singular image of success, which can be harmful to students.

Reducing Stereotype Threat

Stereotypes are woven into the fabric of our education system. However, students can overcome stereotype threat and reduce self-fulfilling prophecies through effective interventions. Students who identify with groups who have been marginalized or disadvantaged may be especially vulnerable to stereotype threat. The following are several research-based tactics you can use as an educator to reduce or eliminate the impact of stereotype threat and create a more equitable learning environment.

- **Provide positive role models**—Many students of color rarely see individuals who look like them in their textbooks or in leadership positions at their schools. However, research has shown that when individuals are given opportunities to interact with successful people from their same social group, they begin to develop a mindset that they also can achieve success. Consider how you can find literature that highlights people of color and their contributions to the discipline you are teaching.

- **Inspire self-affirmation**—Engaging students in self-affirming journaling activities has contributed to a reduction in opportunity gaps in education. Research has shown that students who participated in self-affirmation exercises were more likely to choose a rigorous curriculum in high school, enroll in college, and complete a four-year degree.

- **Develop a growth mindset**—Teach students that the challenges they experience in academic tasks are a normal part of the learning process. Affirm that many students struggle, and you are willing to help them overcome challenges. Show them that you believe that they can be successful. Research has shown that students who were taught a growth mindset had greater enjoyment of the academic process, greater engagement, and higher GPAs than their peers.

- **Talk to students about stereotype threat**—Explicitly talk to students about stereotype threat. Reassure students that if they feel anxiety during academic tasks, it may be because of negative stereotypes associated with their group that have nothing to do with their actual ability to perform well. When students who are knowledgeable about stereotype threat experience anxiety during a task, they can better disassociate their anxiety from their ability by attributing it to stereotype threat and reducing its effect on their performance.

Arming Yourself to Debunk Stereotypes

How can educators arm themselves to debunk negative stereotypes? This resource offers practical tips for advocates who want to equip themselves with the tools necessary to recognize and counteract bad statistics and harmful stereotypes.

- **Calibrate your belief system**—Commit to believing in your students and their capacity to achieve great things.
- **Remain solution-oriented and resist the temptation to magnify the problem**—Refocus the conversation on solutions whenever the magnitude of the problem starts to eclipse the promise of potential solutions.
- **Be willing to admit your own deficiencies**—Acknowledge how your practices or implicit biases may be contributing to the problem or exacerbating it.
- **Interrogate the statistics**—Look for validity in the research. Ask yourself what you do not understand about the statistic and search for clarification.
- **Centralize compassion and care**—Spend time developing meaningful relationships with your students. When you

prioritize care, you automatically resist buying into negative stereotypes about your students, and you are motivated to challenge them.

- **Challenge definitions of commonly used terms**— Concepts like "achievement" and "success" can have multiple meanings. It is important to understand how studies define these terms to understand the narrative behind the statistics.

- **Focus on students' talents, not weaknesses**—If you readily can perceive and communicate your students' strengths and capabilities, it will be easier to recognize and reject statistics that counter this narrative.

- **Analyze your discipline policies**—Take a critical look at the disciplinary procedures within your school or division. Seek to identify the ways in which these policies may contribute to the formation of negative stereotypes or bad statistics.

- **Listen to students**—Ask students what they want from school and how they feel within the school environment. Student voices are the most powerful tool available to combat negative stereotypes about each other.

- **Study success stories**—Adopting a lens of success will empower you to reframe the narrative of bad statistics. Identify individuals, schools, and communities that are defying the stereotypes, and look for strategies to replicate their success.

Conclusion

Setting classroom norms for dialogue is helpful as an educator. It helps students to understand the protocols in place to allow them to speak in a friendly manner while being respectful of others. The words we allow to be said in class matter just as much as teaching students to express themselves.

Sometimes, our beliefs may allow stereotypes to creep into the way we receive communication from students. Focus on the context of the communication happening in your class and listen to your students. We don't always need to have complete control of everything being said. Sometimes, listening is the best way to learn about how your students feel about their lived experiences.

Promote a Decolonial Atmosphere

Our educational system today has established norms that have been in place since the Industrial Revolution. The original educational system wasn't created for folks like me. It wasn't created for women either. These norms were created by white men for white men, and we still hold onto a system that was designed to keep the elite in power and everyone else at the bottom. There's a lot of ideology from Western mindsets that has continued to perpetuate within our educational system. This chapter discusses ways we can decolonize our classrooms.

Coloniality in Education Today

When we say we're going to *decolonize* education, we're planning to disrupt the status quo. One of the things I noticed when I spoke to many of my indigenous students was that they tended to have their heads down. They wouldn't look me in the eye, and that made me curious. I spoke to one of the indigenous staff on campus and told them my situation. I said, "I noticed that many of the students keep their heads down when I'm speaking to them; you wouldn't happen to notice the same thing when you speak to them?" The staff member responded with "In our culture, we view adults/elders as wise, so we show our respect by bowing our head. That's our way of showing respect; now if a student is looking at you in the eye, you may want to see why that is the case."

We live in a time when popular culture and "it's always been that way" dominate what society deems acceptable and normal. However, the challenge is that those who determine what is traditional, normal, popular, or acceptable do not reflect a diverse representation of identities. Many countries in Asia and Africa revere their elders, and younger people utilize culture-specific titles when speaking to their elders. Some countries in Asia bow to each other, and some European countries (France, Italy, Spain) air kiss on the cheek. These are signs of respect in these cultures.

I'll give you another example. Growing up in school, I remember taking music class. I love music and enjoyed learning about various composers and the different eras of music. When we got to classical music, I learned about Beethoven, Mozart, Bach, Chopin, Tchaikovsky, etc. These men are considered some of the greatest classical music composers of all time. But to whom? I would argue that classical music for me should include Negro Spirituals. Also, were there not any women composers during this era? I never learned about Fanny J. Crosby, a blind hymn writer and poetess during the 1800s. Fanny wrote many songs that are sung in churches today such as "Blessed Assurance" and "Pass Me Not, O Gentle Saviour." I guess folks like me don't have a say in who gets included in conversations about the greatest classical musicians.

In the United States, we tend to expect everyone to learn how to speak English and assimilate to the traditional approaches of behavior norms that the dominant culture dictates. If you go against these norms, you are considered weird, different, and sometimes disrespectful. We see examples of these attitudes in school when students are taught how to walk, talk, and interact with each other according to how the adults in the building would like them to behave. However, are those expectations created with their students' identities and talents in mind? "Oh, but we've always done things this way" can't be the reason behind it. Just because you've always done something doesn't make it right. It's time to promote a decolonized atmosphere.

Decoloniality

Let's look at the word *decoloniality*. According to Future Learn, decoloniality is "A movement that identifies the ways in which Western modes of thought and systems of knowledge have been universalized. Decoloniality seeks to move away from this Eurocentrism by focusing on recovering 'alternative' or non-Eurocentric ways of knowing." As a former history teacher, I can attest to my disagreement with some of the ways I was expected to teach certain historical events. I never agreed with the rationale for the Lewis and Clark Expedition. We celebrate the expansion of what we call the United States and share one side of the story. We glorify names such as Meriwether Lewis and William Clark and admire their ability to study the terrain, plants, and animal life. We are taught to admire how they facilitated the establishment of trade opportunities with the local native tribes they encountered. However, we don't mention the impact of their "expedition" on the native communities and the generational effects many of our indigenous communities have faced because of this blatant reconnaissance mission, but we celebrate historical events like this as important milestones.

The Legacy of Colonial Education

We can go all the way back to 1779 when Thomas Jefferson proposed an educational system with two tracks. In his words, he described the tracks as being destined for "the laboring and the learned." What I find interesting is that even in 1779, coded language was utilized. Think about what Jefferson said. He called them "the laboring and the learned." What do you think that means? Who's in the laboring group, and who's in the learned department? Who did these categorizations represent in 1779?

Today, what terminology do we use to express ideas like this? We'll say stuff like "Title I schools," "inner city schools," or "inner city students." We still utilize coded language. This is not new. Another thing that Thomas Jefferson added meant that scholarship would allow a very few of the laboring class to advance by "raking a few geniuses from the rubbish."

We're going to set up these two tracks with the laboring and the learned, and on top of that, we'll just rake in a few geniuses. Within that laboring pot, Jefferson felt that there were a few geniuses. He didn't want them to miss out on any opportunities. Again, he was using coded language. It sounds familiar to me. Let me step on a soapbox for just a moment. It sounds a little familiar when we think about our gifted and talented programs. How does that look? Well, when we think about the representation in our gifted and talented programs, who's there? Are the laboring and the learned there? When we think about how students get recommended into programs such as gifted and talented, we must consider that as teachers and counselors, we're gatekeepers. We control the representation that is in those programs. Black and Brown students and students of color in general are not represented in our gifted and talented programs.

Let's fast-forward to the 1830s. By this time, most Southern states had laws forbidding individuals to teach people in slavery to read. Even so, around 5 percent become literate at great personal risk to themselves. In 1864, Congress made it illegal for Native Americans to be taught in their native languages. Native children as young as four years old were taken from their parents and sent to the Bureau of Indian Affairs off-reservation boarding schools whose goal, as one BIA official put it, was "Kill the Indian in him, and save the man." Indigenous folks had their hair shaved. They weren't allowed to speak their native tongues as if whatever language they spoke was a foreign language. Keep in mind that English is a foreign language. Only in America would we think that it's more important for us to make sure that we preserve the English language. If you're not from England, then you're not speaking English.

Industrial Revolution 1865–1900

The Industrial Revolution was from 1865 to 1900. Surely, things have changed since 150 years ago. Tell me if any of this sounds familiar: Education was managed from the top down. Education was outcome-oriented with aged-based classrooms. Schools predominately had a liberal arts curriculum, and they focused on producing results. That surely doesn't sound like what education looks like today. It's different now, right?

How Can I Begin to Decolonize My Classroom?

My goal is to create a sense of urgency about the need to decolonize our classrooms, and I hope I've persuaded you. Colonialism persists in the lingering ideologies and patterns of power within the American educational system. To facilitate culturally sustaining classrooms and meet the needs of our students, we must centralize multicultural education. Here are some steps to begin decolonizing your classroom that you can implement in any content area and at any grade level:

- Analyze texts and experiences from multiple perspectives and lenses.
- Require students to think about how knowledge is constructed.
- Shift marginalized voices to the center of your curriculum.
- Invite students to think critically and acknowledge biases.

- Promote research and learning via exploration and discussion.
- Allow students to create relevant, authentic learning products.
- Adopt cultural storytelling and include narratives from diverse authors.
- Use inclusive vocabulary and challenge noninclusive or offensive terms.
- Empower students to make decisions about social and political issues.
- Challenge students to use their learning to take action and solve problems.
- Implement transdisciplinary approaches, such as project-based learning.
- Invite students to share how they experience their world and their communities.
- Honor culturally rich modes of expression and ways of working.
- Know and love your students for who they are, not who they might be.

Five Additional Essentials to Decolonizing the Classroom

Dr. Michael Dominguez was a guest on the Leading Equity Podcast entitled "How to Decolonize Your Classroom: Five Essentials Every Teacher Must Know" (https://www.leadingequitycenter .com/86). Here are the five essentials he discussed:

- **Essential 1**—Find literature written by a decolonialized scholar. When we think, "Okay, I want to be better as a culturally responsive educator. I want to show I can support my students better," but I use books that aren't written by folks with lived experiences. We undermine our goals. The first step to decolonize our schools is to find literature written by a decolonial scholar. (We will discuss this more in Chapter 7.)

- **Essential 2**—Spend time with students outside of school settings. Recognize the importance of spending time with families outside school settings. Now, I know for two years we've been in a pandemic. It's tough. It's rough. Shoot, I'm at home. I'm ready to go travel. Spending time with families outside of school settings is not ideal. It's not feasible these times, but if there are ways that you can attend a quinceanera, a bar mitzvah, or a powwow, I recommend doing that. I am not limiting you to attend only cultural events as mentioned in Chapter 3. There are extracurricular activities, such as sports, debate teams, chess teams, cheerleading teams, and so on.

- **Essential 3**—Build curriculum around authentic transdisciplinary problems. How relevant is the content that you're presenting to your students? Can your students identify within their own community the content that's happening to them?

- **Essential 4**—Check your language practices. Are we allowing our students to be themselves? Are we allowing them to speak the language that they prefer to speak? I believe in the value of academic language such as Standard English. I believe that there's a time and a place when we want to be able to express ourselves in a formal way. However, we also don't want to diminish our students' identities, and I'll even expand that to our families and our staff. We don't want to diminish their opportunities to be themselves through their use of a variety of nonstandard English that makes them comfortable. (Refer to Chapter 4 for more information about checking your language practices.)

- **Essential 5**—Know and love your students for who they are. How important is this? I mean, we often hear, "Oh, it's very important to develop relationships with our families if we want them to be engaged." When we think about the experiences of our family members, we might have parents or guardians who have gone to the school. They may be alumni of the school, and maybe they didn't have the best experience. We wonder why they don't want to come. How are we providing a welcoming experience for our students and their families when we say that we're going to empower them for anti-racist practices? This is not a time to set up a session or a parent night to tell our parents how to be culturally responsive at home. That doesn't make any sense to me. How are you going to tell a family how to be culturally responsive?

Making the Shift Away from Banking

In *Pedagogy of the Oppressed*, author Paulo Freire (1968) mentions the concept of the banking system. The banking concept views learning as a process in which students simply store the information given to them by their teachers. The following is a list of mindsets and instructional strategies that you can adopt to combat the banking paradigm and facilitate a learning experience that is dynamic and engaging for all students.

Mindsets	Instructional Strategies
My students' views of the world matter in my classroom.	I can position myself as the facilitator of the learning experience, rather than as the keeper of all knowledge.
	I can invite my students to build on their prior knowledge to enhance their new learning.

Mindsets	Instructional Strategies
Learning in my classroom is an active process, not a passive one.	I can activate students' critical thinking skills by empowering them to generate their own questions, rather than simply answering mine. I can leverage the processes and tools that professionals use to allow my students to apply their knowledge to authentic tasks.
Effective teaching and learning in my classroom require two-way communication.	I can ask for my students' feedback on my lesson plans and my lesson implementation. I can provide my students with opportunities to make meaningful choices about their learning.
My classroom procedures and norms should support students assuming the roles of active, authentic learners.	I can use discussion protocols that honor each student's voice and contribution. I can co-construct classroom norms and ways of working with my students.
I teach most effectively when I am willing to learn from my students and capitalize on their strengths.	I can use a reciprocal teaching model to empower my students to support each other's learning. I can allow my students to personalize their learning experience by incorporating their backgrounds, interests, and identities.

Transitioning from Oppression to Elevation

In what ways do we intentionally and unintentionally oppress or discriminate against our students? This resource will empower you to take a deep look into the way our schools and classrooms operate to identify oppressive or discriminatory policies that may be impacting students daily. Use the following tips to begin making the shift from unintentional oppression to intentional elevation.

Tip #1: Acknowledge That Oppression Exists

Acknowledge that the American education system was not set up to support the success of students of color. As a result, opportunity gaps continue to impact Hispanic, Native American, and Black students. Take a critical look at your school's policies and procedures. Do any of them impact certain groups more than others? For instance, does the dress code penalize girls more harshly than boys? Do disciplinary policies lead to a disproportionate number of referrals for students of color? Consider gathering student and family feedback about the student handbook and school policies. Acknowledge that there may be systems in place within your school that are inequitable. Keep in mind that silence and complacency send a clear message to students that their needs are unimportant.

Tip #2: Listen to Your Students

Students' voices are essential in developing a culture of elevation. Students should feel as though they have choices and their concerns are heard. Involve your students in the implementation of school policies and procedures. If your school does not have a student council or a similar representative body, consider starting one! Students should have representation in the planning and development processes of the decisions that impact them. Excluding or overlooking student voices may perpetuate oppressive experiences for them.

Tip # 3: Inspire Students to Learn

Focus on processes of learning that are affirming, rather than forcing students to be compliant and prioritizing quantitative end results. To what extent are students able to exercise agency in how their classes or schools are run? Consider allowing your students to help you co-create engaging learning experiences that welcome their ideas and interests as they relate to the course content.

Conclusion

Reflect on who your students are and how they engage with the world. Allow them to bring those talents and skills to address issues and problems that relate to them. Teach from a social justice perspective by embedding content that resonates with students' experiences and issues that are important to them. Go beyond discussing the historical trauma that people of color have experienced such as slavery, genocide, conquistador exploration, and other areas of oppression. Presenting groups exclusively in the context of historical oppression only perpetuates a dominant/non-dominant dynamic between majorities and minorities. This essentially rubs salt in a wound. It sends a message to students of color that in the eyes of society, their identities rest on vulnerability to authority. Instead, bring in aspects of their cultural identities that address the daily experiences of students of color. Students also need to see the triumphs and successes of their people and understand how those people gained power.

Avoid the exploitation of cultures and deficit perspectives that maintain colonial patterns of power. Instead, help students learn in culturally congruent ways. Help students learn about science, literature, and history from individuals who look like them as the focal point rather than use traditional methods of content that are dominated by whiteness.

Answer the Following Questions:

1. Are my students' behaviors in line with my views of how students are supposed to behave and interact with one another?

   _____

2. Am I operating on a "you got to learn this for the test" mindset, or am I bringing in culturally relevant content to engage my students and develop their critical thinking skills?

   _____

3. In what ways have I ventured beyond my textbook, and is the content in the book indicative of my classroom demographics?

   _____

4. What indicator in each of my lesson plans illustrates my attention to culturally relevant teaching?

   _____

Equity-minded educators actively work to ensure their students can see themselves within the course content. If you truly value diversity and student voice, it can't happen through the occasional culturally based holiday or activity (e.g., Hispanic Heritage Month, Black History Month, Native American History Month). Instead, culturally relevant teaching must be a daily practice woven into the fabric of the coursework in which students regularly experience lessons that reflect their language and cultural identity. Go beyond observable and concrete measures such as food, music, dress, posters, and books. Those are important and exciting to students, but do not stop there. You can do better, and you can dig more deeply.

A significant attribute of equity is the ability to recognize culture and learn how students' culture impacts their beliefs and behaviors. Consider the unconscious associations of students in their behavior and demeanor. For example, ponder the ways in which students interact with each other outside the classroom such as during recess and lunch (settings such as these allow you to learn from students without the expectations of traditional classroom behavior). What are the norms of their social interactions? What are their communication styles? Consider their behaviors and compare them to what you and the school culture consider acceptable and normal.

Adopt an Advocacy Mentality

Advocates play an instrumental role in transforming the landscape of education and maximizing all students' educational experience. As you continue this journey, be advised that advocating for equity is not a one-time declaration. Advocacy is a long-term commitment to a way of existing and working within the world of education. It will require consistently setting high expectations for all students, fighting for representation in all aspects of curriculum and instruction, and adopting culturally sustaining teaching practices. It requires deep reflection, tough conversations, and a willingness to challenge traditional methods. This chapter outlines several commitments you can make now to adopt an advocacy mentality.

Commit to Understanding What It Means to Be an Advocate

What is an advocate? An advocate is someone who recognizes that we do not live in a just society. Advocates are not comfortable with the status quo and are willing to speak up on behalf of others. As you begin to position yourself as an advocate for equity in education, it is crucial to recognize two critical advocacy characteristics.

First, being an advocate is a long-term decision. There is no book, seminar, or professional development session that instantly will transform you into an advocate. You are embarking on a life-long process of deep learning, active self-discovery, and critical analysis of the world around you. *Advocacy is not for the faint of heart! It's supposed to be hard.*

Second, advocacy is a full-time commitment. It requires great courage and a willingness to renew that commitment every single day. Advocating for equity is more than being open to new ideas or appreciating diversity. It requires more than creating a safe space for students in your classroom. While these things are good first steps in embracing an equity mindset, dedicated advocacy requires a willingness to stand up and speak out on behalf of others whenever and wherever injustice exists.

Ask yourself:

- Think of an individual, past or present, who you would classify as an advocate. What characteristics or behaviors help you identify this person as an advocate?

- Now, consider your own identity and background. What talents, traits, or privileges might uniquely position *you* to be an advocate?

- Take a moment to visualize your current context. What could advocacy look like in your classroom, school, organization, or community? How could it sound? What effect might it have on others?

Commit to Establishing Your "Why"

Every educator has a unique story behind why they chose to enter the profession. Many of us were inspired by exceptional teachers in our lives. Some of us have just always had a knack for helping others to learn. Some of us pursued other careers only to realize that teaching is our true calling. However, your story begins, there is something that drives you to do what you do every day. As an advocate, you must understand *why* you became an educator and how this reason compels you to advocate for equity.

Once you have established your reason confidently for being an educator-advocate, carefully consider the extent to which that motivation manifests itself in your profession. Think about your teaching practices. Do those practices challenge harmful ways of thinking, or do they perpetuate systems of oppression? Do your students' languages, cultures, and identities have value in your school or your classroom? How do you strive to communicate that worth to them? How culturally responsive is your instruction? Does a socially just lens inform your approach to teaching and learning?

As equity advocates, we must reflect continually on how we show up in teaching and learning spaces. We need to be aware of how our backgrounds, experiences, cultures, and identities influence our position as educators and advocates. Once we can be confident in our purpose, we can commit to letting that purpose shine through our practice.

Ask yourself:

- What led you to become an educator? Reflect on the experiences, individuals, and interactions that motivated you to enter the profession.

- Complete the following sentence: When students walk into my school or my classroom, I want them to feel. . . . What steps have you taken to create this environment? What additional measures might you take?

- What is your mission as an educator? Try to take this mission and distill it into 10 words or less. Challenge yourself to internalize this statement as your daily mantra.

Commit to Educating Yourself

Advocacy occurs within a context that is both complex and dynamic. Advocacy is part of a complex historical narrative that exists alongside deep-rooted traditions of injustice and discrimination particularly within our education systems. How much do you personally know about the history of social justice in American schools? How much do you know about the educational equity issues that plague the global community? Are you aware of the equity and social justice issues that have existed in your community?

To be equipped effectively as advocates, we, as educators, must take the time to learn intentionally about the rich legacy of advocacy including the battles fought against segregation, cultural discrimination, and inequitable funding. This knowledge will not only enable you to think critically about the societal and systemic factors that contribute to inequitable school environments, but also it will empower you to be a better advocate for all students.

There are many ways to educate yourself as an advocate, and the Leading Equity Center is a great start! As you continue learning and seeking out information, however, be sure to consider multiple narratives. Recognize that the dominant discourse may exclude good perspectives from individuals and groups that have been marginalized historically. Use the information you gather to better understand the trauma that has impacted individuals in your community and more fully appreciate your own position within the tradition of educational advocacy.

Ask yourself:

- What do I already know about the legacy of advocacy in education? What do I want to know?
- How can I find the information I am seeking? How might I document what I have learned?
- What actions do I intend to take because of my learning? What will I do when new questions arise?

Commit to Recognizing When Race and Social Inequities Are Present in the Classroom and Beyond

If we are honest, sometimes it can be challenging to recognize when and where inequities exist especially when they are not in the form of blatant discrimination. It also can be significantly different when they do not affect us personally and *especially* difficult when we are perpetrators of those inequities. As with most elements of your equity journey, you should start your examination with yourself. Take a good long look at who you are as an educator. Be honest about your implicit biases and critically analyze how those biases might show up in your instructional practices. Know that even the most well-intentioned teachers can fall into the trap of disrupting cultures or marginalizing identities through their pedagogy. To remain sensitive to your instructional approach's effects, pay attention to how your students communicate their experiences in your classroom. Be open to hearing their honest feedback and use that feedback to make constructive changes in your practice.

Equity advocates must work to guarantee safe spaces in our classrooms; however, that is not where our work stops! What happens when your students move to the next classroom? How will you ensure that their experiences remain equitable? Advocacy requires that we commit to taking a stand that extends beyond what is within our immediate control. Once you have created an equitable learning space in your classroom, look at your school wholistically. Actively engage in transforming your school's culture by questioning inequitable practices and policies. Be brave enough to challenge those policies and support a critical revision of them. Push for the inclusion of diverse perspectives and marginalized voices in conversations about what is best for students.

One last thing to keep in mind is that our work as advocates, just like our work as educators, does not stop when we step outside our school buildings. If you have chosen a commitment to advocacy, then you are deciding to adopt a way of existing within the world that requires you to look closely and think deeply about society at large. Understand that a student's experience within a school building is not a suspension of the real world. Societal, cultural, and systemic factors impact a student's existence both in school and outside school. How can you use your position as a leader in education to advocate for student learning and achievement and students' safety, wellness, and joy beyond the school building walls?

Ask yourself:

- Even young students can articulate when they feel that something is wrong or unfair; they may not express those feelings in the language of equity. Think about the students you teach. What words or phrases might they use to indicate that they've witnessed or experienced something inequitable?

- Consider your school's culture. Think about aspects such as discipline, representation, academic programs, and leadership opportunities. How might instances of inequity look or sound in your school?

- What factors in society might influence the way students experience school? As an educator, how might you remain aware of the issues beyond school that impact your students?

Commit to Addressing Equity Issues Intentionally and Proactively

Once you have identified an equity issue in your classroom, school, or community, what is the best way to address it? Unfortunately, there is no magical cure for injustice or inequity. Furthermore, any way that you choose to take a stand will require some degree of vulnerability or discomfort. You may find yourself needing to initiate brave conversations with your students, your colleagues, your friends, or perhaps even your supervisors. The best step you can take to prepare yourself as an advocate is to get comfortable with being uncomfortable. Know that you do not need to have all the answers. You can start just by asking the right questions.

Issues such as racism, bias, and discrimination are not going to subside unless advocates like you and me affirm and reaffirm our commitment to confront injustice. We must be intentional about participating in the meaningful dialogue that educates others and raises awareness about our students' equity issues both in school and in life. These conversations will play a key role in helping to shift our schools toward a culture of equity. As an advocate, keep in mind that you do not have to wait until an issue arises to speak up on behalf of your students. You can start building a culture of equity proactively in your school today!

Ask yourself:

- Take a moment to think about your personal interactions outside of school. When do you have conversations about equity and inequity? Who is involved in these conversations? How comfortable do you feel initiating and navigating these conversations?

- Now, reflect on your current learning environment. When and where are conversations about equity *encouraged* within your classroom or school?

- What discussion norms might you need in place to participate fully in brave conversations about equity and inequity? What models might your *students* need to feel empowered to have these conversations?

Commit to Supporting Student Advocacy

One of the most powerful actions you can take as an advocate is to teach your students how to advocate for themselves and each other. In today's complex society, students not only need the skills to analyze academic content and texts critically, but they also need the skills to think critically about the behaviors and interactions that occur within the world around them. You can start equipping students for advocacy by teaching them language and strategies they can use to discuss complex concepts such as race, identity, justice, and power.

Supporting student-led advocacy groups is another avenue that you can take to encourage and empower students in your school community to remain actively engaged in equity work. If student-led advocacy groups already exist in your school, consider how you might support their work. For example, you may be able to serve as a mentor, help amplify students' voices throughout the school or community, or even advocate for additional resources and support from leaders or organizations. If student-led advocacy groups do not exist in your school, consider introducing your students to examples of how individuals their age have made a meaningful difference in society.

Keep in mind that, as educators, the knowledge and skills that we teach to students ultimately should be in the service of making the world a better, more just place for everyone. Take a moment to consider your curriculum. Do students experience empowerment through the lessons that you teach? Are they encouraged to view themselves as agents of change who can make a difference in their communities? Commit to teaching your students how they can leverage their knowledge and skills to disrupt unjust systems and promote equity for all.

Ask yourself:

- Think about your educational journey as a student. When did you learn about equity and justice? Did these lessons occur formally in classrooms or informally in other spaces?
- Think about the curriculum and content that you teach. How might the knowledge and skills in your curriculum connect to equity?
- What additional support might you need to leverage your curriculum to support student advocacy?

Often, race and social inequities are present in the classroom, yet race and social inequities are difficult for many educators to discuss. As a result, these issues rarely are addressed with intentionality, and students from marginalized backgrounds continue to face oppressive practices that minimize and suppress their identities on a regular basis. Instead, you must engage actively in investigating inequitable practices among colleagues and school policies and do not stand on the sideline hoping that someone else will say something; students will not thrive if you adopt a passive approach.

Five Simple Ways to Introduce Students to Advocacy

In today's digital world, students are surrounded by advocacy. Because of this, the classroom can be a critical space for educators to help students understand the context of advocacy, and teachers can empower students to take a stand for their beliefs. Here are five simple ways that you can introduce students to advocacy:

- **Have conversations that matter in the classroom**—As you teach the knowledge and skills of your curriculum, find ways to connect this content to the most meaningful, relevant aspects of students' lives. Help students see the connections between what they are learning in school and what they experience in the world beyond school.

- **Examine examples of knowledge-driven advocacy**— Identify individuals who have leveraged their knowledge or skills in a particular field to effect change or promote equity. Allow students to explore the various ways in which research and scholarship have led to positive changes in society.

- **Encourage students' passions**—Provide students with the safety and support to discover their beliefs and passions. Expose them to new ideas and teach them the skills to challenge, extend, and amplify those ideas.

- **Meet students on their terms**—According to Dr. Yolanda Sealey-Ruiz, "The internet is the new grassroots place to organize" (https://www.leadingequitycenter.com/178). Embrace your students as digital natives. Provide them with the language to discuss and critique instances of advocacy to which they are already exposed via social media and other online platforms.

- **Amplify student voices**—Create frequent and meaningful opportunities for students to share their ideas with an audience beyond the classroom. Cultivate spaces in which they can build confidence in their own voices and learn to appreciate their value that they can share with the world.

Ask yourself:

- What teaching practices am I utilizing that challenge traditional forms of teaching?

- To what extent are my actions displaying to my students that I value their language, culture, and identities?

- In what ways have I critically practiced culturally responsive teaching through a socially just lens?

Invest in meaningful dialogue that brings awareness to issues students from marginalized backgrounds are facing in school. Such dialogue can bring about heightened socio-cultural consciousness. Furthermore, equity-focused teachers instruct their students on *how* to discuss equity and social justice. These are learned concepts, and teachers can help their students develop awareness and advocacy skills because students also need to learn how to advocate for themselves and others.

Empowering Students to Advocate for Learning Supports

Creating an equitable learning environment requires us to ensure that all students have access to the learning supports they need to be successful. How can we, as educators, accurately identify what students need to learn best? We might consider turning to the experts—students themselves! This resource provides five tips that you can leverage to empower your students to identify and advocate for the supports that will maximize their learning and achievement:

- **Expose students to various methods of learning**—In many traditional school settings, there is little variation in the learning processes that are conducted within classrooms daily. Students often are encouraged to rely on reading texts, listening to lectures, and taking notes as a primary means of learning content. However, exposing students to new and varied ways of learning such as inquiry, problem-solving, prototyping, and research will allow them to think more critically about the processes that work best for them in any given learning situation.

- **Ensure that a variety of learning supports are readily available to all students**—Keep in mind that many of the accessibility tools that are beneficial to students with special needs may be beneficial to all individuals at some point in time. As you plan learning activities, consider how you might embed learning supports for all students in a way that empowers them to make meaningful choices about their learning while preserving their privacy and dignity.

- **Normalize the use of learning supports in the classroom**—Students need to understand that all learners make use of tools and strategies to help them attain new concepts and skills. For instance, one student may choose to sit near the front of the room to see the board better. Another may choose to sit near the back of the room so they don't disrupt others if they need to stand or pace. Help students understand that we all make choices that can either contribute to or detract from our ability to learn effectively.

- **Model the use of learning supports as an educator**—Not only do students need to see their peers of all ability levels selecting and incorporating learning supports, they also need to see adults effectively doing the same! As an educator, you can help students take ownership over their learning path by being explicit about when and why you choose to use your own learning supports. For example, you might think aloud as you are reading a text to explain to students how you benefit from highlighting main ideas.

- **Guide students through intentional reflections on learning processes and outcomes**—The key to empowering students to select appropriate learning supports during various learning situations is giving them the time and space to reflect on those decisions. Students need to make connections between the learning decisions they make and their experiences and outcomes as learners. Allow students to think critically about their choices and encourage them to try new strategies until they find what works best for them!

A strong student group that is organized with a mission and objectives goes a long way when it comes to challenging institutional practices that are unjust toward certain groups. On local and national scales, have students engage in lessons that address controversial topics such as mass incarceration, police brutality, civil rights, immigration, racial profiling, healthcare disparities, unequal pay issues, trauma, suicide, drug abuse, women's rights, and privilege. Have students discuss and question the contributing factors to these issues and teach them to think critically about how these issues impact them and other people personally.

Further Supporting Student Advocates

This section offers practical suggestions for educators who are working to support student advocacy. The following considerations provide key actions that you can take to empower and motivate students to amplify their voices:

- **Let students lead**—Position yourself as a guide, not a leader, as your students seek to create change in their schools and communities. This may require you to shift from a position of authority to allow students the space and opportunity to take ownership of their pursuit of social justice.

- **Support students in connecting and amplifying**—As students identify and confront injustices within their communities, help them see connections between their work and the work of other student-led groups or community-based organizations. These connections may serve to amplify their message of social justice and give them access to broader platforms or additional resources.

- **Help students see what's possible**—Use your perspective as an adult to help students situate their efforts within a rich global history of social justice movements. Help them see patterns within traditions of advocacy so they can understand better what is truly possible within their communities and what changes are taking place around the world.

- **Allow students to engage in productive struggle**—As educators, we are predisposed to want to help students find the right answers. However, as you support student advocates, it is much more powerful to allow students to engage in a productive struggle around complex issues. Empower students to make decisions, ask questions, and challenge each other in a way that moves the conversation forward.

- **Provide a safe space for processing complex emotions**—Keep in mind that advocacy is emotionally taxing work for anyone. Ensure that you consistently can offer your student advocates a safe space to process complex emotions that may result from experiencing setbacks, suffering loss, or witnessing trauma within the community.

- **Be available**—The most impactful thing that we can do as educators to support student advocates is to be available. Let your students know that you care about them as individuals and you support their dreams and goals. Send a consistent message that their safety, wellness, and success matter deeply to you.

Questions to Spark Students' Thinking About Race, Equity, and Social Justice

Multicultural education is not just about helping students of color see themselves within the curriculum. In fact, it is important for *all* students to engage in thinking and learning about race, equity, and social justice especially in schools where the student population is mostly white.

The questions listed in this section can prompt students' thinking about concepts related to social justice at three different levels:

- **What?** Unpacking complex concepts relating to race, equity, and social justice

- **So what?** Examining the impact of words and behaviors on individuals and communities

- **Now what?** Locating oneself within the movement toward a socially just world

Educators may choose to integrate these questions within learning activities as self-reflection opportunities, journaling exercises, or even small group discussion prompts.

What?

These questions invite students to unpack complex concepts relating to race, equity, and social justice.

- Race is part of a person's identity. What are other aspects or pieces of a person's identity?

- What is your culture or cultural identity? (Try to think beyond just your race!)

- What do you know about your family's ancestry or history?
- How often do you think about your own race or culture?
- When is race relevant in your life?
- What does it mean to be "color-blind"?
- Why does race matter?
- Think about the student population at your school. How diverse is it? (You might think about family income, gender, sexual orientation, religion, language, or other aspects.)
- Have you ever felt mistreated or excluded?
- How do you identify when something is unjust?
- What do you believe is true without a doubt?

So What?

These questions invite students to examine the impact of words and behaviors on individuals and communities.

- Think about the people you interact with daily. How are these people like you? How are they different?
- Think about the individuals you learn about in school. How are those individuals like you? How are they different?
- When and where do you talk about race at school? When and where are you *encouraged* to talk about race? Why do you think that is?
- Look at the images in your immediate classroom surroundings. (Try looking at textbook pictures, posters, books covers, etc.) Do the pictures represent your culture?
- How "normal" is it to see your culture, race, or background represented in the content you learn in school? (Think about textbooks, test questions, posters and handouts, or other educational materials.)

- What common phrases include the words *black* or *white*? Which phrases are positive? Which phrases are negative?

- Where do you get information about what's going on in the world? Whose stories are told the with the most emphasis?

- Does your race impact the way you live your life? Have you seen people's race have an impact on the way they live their lives?

- What emotions do you feel when you see racism or injustice?

Now What?

These questions challenge students to locate themselves within the movement toward a socially just world:

- What people or groups do you influence?
- What privileges do you think you have?
- What access and opportunities do you think you have?
- When do you have conversations about race? Who is involved in those conversations? Are those conversations comfortable or uncomfortable for you?
- What do you know about cultures other than your own? How could you increase your knowledge?
- How can you identify when injustice occurs within your own community?
- What are the risks of standing up for what's right?
- What would you say is your responsibility?
- How can you create a change in your community?

Students need to experience empowerment and view themselves as change agents who can make a difference in their community. Teach them how they can get involved and contribute to disrupting damaging behaviors that are normal and acceptable in their school and community.

Commit to Connecting with Other Equity Advocates

The commitment you have made to advocate for equity is one of the most important steps you can take as an educator to improve all students' experiences. However, advocacy can, at times, be challenging and isolating. Together, we can make a powerful impact if we continue to connect, learn from each other, and encourage each other. How might you connect with other educators who are advocates for equity? You may be able to find colleagues within your school or district who are committed to ensuring equitable experiences for students. Additionally, you can connect with advocates around the country through networks like the Leading Equity Center.

Remember that you are not alone in your commitment to equity. The Leading Equity Center's commitment to you is to support you in this journey! Connect with us at any time.

Ask yourself:

- What opportunities exist within your school or division for educators to connect and collaborate around issues of equity? How might you get involved in these opportunities?
- Think about your professional learning network. How might you expand your network to include other equity-minded professionals?
- How might the Leading Equity Center support you in your work? Remember that you can connect with us any time.

Conclusion

As you read this book, I'm sure that you can think of at least one other person who could benefit from learning ways to be a more equitable educator. Students often interact with multiple teachers and staff throughout the day. Sharing what you have learned and developing relationships with students ultimately help the overall school culture.

Help students feel empowered to be their authentic selves by establishing ways to think critically about social issues that impact their community. There are several commitments that you can make to adopt an advocacy mentality. These commitments include understanding what it means to be an advocate, establishing your "why," educating yourself, recognizing when race and social inequities are present in the classroom and beyond, committing to address equity issues intentionally and proactively, and supporting student advocacy.

Conclusion.

Educate Yourself

I've always tried to learn a little bit about everything. If I'm in a conversation about a topic and I have no clue what's going on, I'm going to go back and research it; I'm going to Google it. I am going to dive in. Maybe that's the PhD part of me, the researcher side of me, or just my thirst for knowledge. Anytime that there's a conversation about something that I do not know, I will do my best to try to learn a little bit about it so the next time that conversation comes up, I will be prepared.

In this chapter, I discuss how you can educate yourself by diving into culturally responsive practices. Remember that culture extends beyond race. I also discuss what it means to be a cultural insider versus a cultural outsider. Finally, I share some tips on how you can take control of your professional development opportunities.

What Interests Your School Stakeholders?

When I moved to Oregon to start a new job as school principal, the parents of some of my students showed up to help me unload. I recall one of the parents got "mad" at me because I had an artificial Christmas tree. The parent was unloading the stuff off the truck, and he saw this artificial Christmas tree. He said, "This is Oregon. What are you doing? How dare you have this artificial tree in freaking Oregon? This is the Christmas tree capital of the world." Okay, I'll admit that he wasn't really mad and was pulling my leg, but it was a reminder of the value of educating myself about the community I was serving.

One of the things I learned from being in Oregon was the significance of forestry. I couldn't tell you how many conversations that I had regarding agriculture, forestry, and just being part of nature. That was kind of like my introduction because this was my first time moving to the Pacific Northwest, and I didn't know a lot about the area.

I'll be honest: initially, it wasn't of interest to me, but again, those conversations would come up so much that you know what I did? Not having a green thumb in this world, I sat there and took the time to do some research on forestry. I learned a little bit about agriculture and gardening and all these things. I did this because these topics were coming up, and it's helpful as a principal, as a school leader, and as part of the school culture to be able to interact with the families and parents of your students about common topics that are relevant to your community.

It's Not Just About Race

Cultural responsiveness is not limited to race. How does culturally responsive teaching look? Culturally responsive teach takes into consideration that there are many cultures within the community I am serving, and I'm going to learn about them.

Again, I'm one of those people who likes to learn a little bit about everything. That's what I do. That leads me to my next point. There is power in educating yourself. Now, I could have sat there and talked to every parent I knew who might be interested or know a little bit about forestry, which was very common where I lived. However, I wanted to educate myself because sometimes when we see people who look a certain way, we assume that an individual might have some sort of knowledge or understanding of a topic because of a stereotype. It might be offensive if that person doesn't know about the topic that I assumed that they should understand. Educate yourself because at the end of the day, it's not someone else's responsibility to educate you. A lot of folks are representatives of groups that have historically been marginalized or underrepresented in many situations, and they become spokespersons for their identities.

The Few, the Proud

My daughter is the only Black girl in her class. It has always been that way throughout the time that she's been in school. Guess what? Oftentimes, she has come home from school and told me, "Daddy, we talked about Africa today. Daddy, we talked about civil rights today. Daddy, we talked about Black history today. All eyes were on me." Imagine how it feels when you're in a classroom of 20 kids and you're the only person of color or you're the only person with a unique identity. Suddenly, here comes a topic centered around your background, ethnicity and culture, language, identity, or sexual orientation. When those conversations come up, everyone is staring at you. Imagine being in second grade and that experience is happening. Imagine being in first grade. Imagine being an adult in a staff meeting and the conversation is happening.

Sometimes, as educators, we're so smart (or covert rather) with some of the language that we utilize. We utilize coded language such as "urban kids" or "street kids." I've heard that before. We won't say specifically who we're addressing, but there's an undercurrent in the language that gives it away. "Okay, I know exactly what you're referencing." Don't refer to a population of students as "inner city." People can pinpoint exactly which family someone is discussing. We don't want to generalize. We don't want to make assumptions. When you want to ask a question without assumptions or stereotypes, you can ask, "Has this been your experience?"

Has This Been Your Experience?

I remember one time when I was at work, one of the staff members asked me a question regarding housing within the community that I was serving. The staff member asked, "Sheldon, was it like that for you when you were in the projects?"

I took a moment to process the question. *How in the world did this person assume that I came from the projects? That has not been my experience.* However, the person looked at me and just assumed that I must be from the hood. One way that she could have reframed that question to me, as opposed to assuming that this is where I was raised, was to ask, "Has this been your experience?" Then, I could say, "You know what? No, it hasn't been my experience. I'm not familiar with it."

One of the things that I've learned from living in the Northwest is a Black child growing up in Oakland, California, and a Black child growing up in the south side of Chicago, Illinois, have different experiences throughout their education, in their neighborhoods, and in their lives than a Black child growing up in rural Idaho. Does that make that individual who grew up in rural Idaho less Black? No. At the end of the day, people don't know where you were raised.

You see me on the street. You see my color. You see who I am, and that's about it. That's all you know. Then, what happens? Those stereotypes start to come in. Those assumptions start to be made. You have only limited information. All we can see is somebody's skin color, and we start to make assumptions. At the end of the day, an individual's experience is that individual's experience. The question you should ask is, "Has this been your experience?"

Cultural Taxation

It is not someone else's responsibility to educate you. Couple that with the idea that we don't want to make assumptions based on stereotypes and limited information. Together, those add up to what's called *cultural taxation*. Cultural taxation means that I represent a group of people. This is my identity, and I'm me. Maybe I'm looked at as a spokesperson. Maybe I am called to do additional work outside the scope of my job responsibilities because no one else is there. For example, I see that a lot of my Latinx folks who work as educators in schools are called in to be translators. An administrator or another staff member comes into the classroom and says, "I'm going to watch your class because we need some translation done." Cultural taxation happens when you're called to translate. Maybe it's not Spanish. Maybe it's a different language, or maybe you're called in to be a mentor to students who represent the same identities as you. Again, you're doing additional jobs for which you're not getting paid. This is not a complaint because my mentality always has been, "If I don't do it, who will?" Additionally, they may have someone asking questions as if they represent the entire community with whom they identify. That also is taxing, and sometimes, this can cause fatigue.

How Does Educating Yourself Look?

It's one thing to say, "I just Googled something. I just found a nice article." You also need to pay attention to who wrote that article, who wrote that book, and who wrote or created that video. You need to evaluate whatever content you are consuming. Does this individual have lived experiences that they can discuss?

Cultural Outsiders vs. Cultural Insiders

Too many times, I've heard conversations or seen articles written by people who do not identify with the community they are discussing. Sure, they did some research. They studied, or they overheard information. Perhaps someone of that community talked to them about it, and now they are reporting it, but they're still cultural outsiders.

What's a cultural outsider? *Cultural outsiders* are individuals who appreciate the culture, but they are not born into it, and it is not a part of their daily experience. I used to love to go to powwows. I used to get invited to powwows, and I still go to powwows every now and then. I enjoy powwows because I love the fellowship. I love the dancing. I love the drums. I love the songs. I love the community. I love the sense of family being together, but because I'm not indigenous, I'm a cultural outsider.

I appreciate a community and culture that I do not represent, and I'm participating in events that are planned, financed, and operated by cultural insiders. However, I'm not a part of the community. I've been asked to judge powwow dances. I'm very familiar with the various categories within dancing. When you're educating yourself, find content that is created by individuals who represent the community they're writing about.

Tokenized Celebrations

When we're thinking about educating ourselves, we need to consider *tokenized celebrations*. Sometimes, when we're at a place where we're saying, "You know what? There's something that I do not know. I want to learn more about this culture. I want to learn more about this practice." However, the reason we want to learn more about these individual celebrations and holidays is that they are individual celebrations. There's Black History Month, or maybe it's Native American Heritage Month. Maybe it's Latinx Heritage Month, Pride Month, or Asian Month. The time of the celebration is coming up, and we want this to be part of our lesson and our content. We might spend a month or a few weeks and do some studying and research, and that's it. We create one lesson. We create one unit. Maybe if we're lucky, we create one unit based on a tokenized celebration that features some celebration or cuisine.

Now, I think it's important that our students learn about various cultures, and I think we're doing our kids a disservice when we don't teach them. Don't make special holidays or months the only times that you try to teach your students about other cultures. Find content written by cultural insiders and study up on it especially if you have representation within your classroom.

Sometimes, I'll hear somebody say, "Oh, well. We have only one or two students of this identity." My answer is, "Where's the threshold? How many more did you need to take this seriously?" I think we can all agree that we want our students to feel welcome. We want them to feel like they are included within the school.

When we think about tokenized celebrations, the impact of those celebrations comes from an oppressive or a negative state. We do some research on the Civil Rights Movement, but what was it? That was people, a group of people of color, Dr. King's "I Have a Dream" speech, and the pursuit of civil rights. If that's the only content that a student is getting or learning about when it comes to various communities, one could argue, "Yes, we got some laws passed back in the '60s for civil rights," but I would argue that the civil rights movement is still happening.

And when we think about what's happening within our country, if you're in the United States, when you're thinking about what's happening in our schools, the movement continues. We don't want to just lean on tragedies. We think about the conquistadors; that's the only history that our students are getting about Spanish and European conquest.

We're doing our kids a disservice. There are some amazing things that various communities, civilizations, have done. But if we don't highlight those things, we don't talk about medicine, inventions, science, technology, engineering, and mathematics from various cultures, and women as well. Again, it's not just a racial thing. But if there's no representation there, we're doing our kids a disservice.

Community Relevance

When it comes to educating yourself, the final bit of advice that I want to add is about the importance of understanding the specific needs of your community. Remember my story regarding my move to the Northwest at the beginning of this chapter? I moved to a community that was tightly connected to the forestry industry, so I learned specifically about what interested my community.

Before I started working on the reservation, I honestly did not know much about indigenous cultures and traditions. Something I learned from working with two tribes that were put on a reservation and forced to sign treaties that have continued to be broken over time was that these tribes had their own languages, their own traditions, and their own culture. Now, over time, you have two indigenous communities that are forced to live together in a small area of land. Naturally, a lot of customs are going to mix. Keeping those traditions is very important to them.

Think about the various tribes and nations that are here; they have their own traditions, their way of life, their culture, and their communities. They're proud. If I read a book on Latinx communities, those communities in California might be different from Latinx communities in Texas. I need to find content written by their own voices. I need to educate myself on the specific needs of my community.

Finding the Right Literature

Find literature to support your learning and understanding of equity. Challenge yourself to read books written about historically marginalized people by their own voices. Find books written beyond the area of education and oppression. Don't settle for books that are meant to make you feel comfortable. Instead, read books that will challenge your level of comfort and confidence.

Approach the literature with an open mind to learn about historically underrepresented groups of people and their experiences. This will help you appreciate the challenges that historically marginalized, specifically, people of color, experience. This also will help you gain a better understanding of what we traditionally view as ways that students should learn, respond, and behave in a classroom, which comes from an assimilated mindset.

Here are some questions I want you to think consider:

- What books have I read on multicultural education and equity?
- How am I actively seeking knowledge to address social justice as a professional?

As an alternative, we need to learn to disrupt the way we approach learning from a one-size-fits-all approach. The way your students exist in this world is different from each other, and it's different for a lot of us as educators.

Many of your students have had to deal with generational issues that continue to suppress their identities, require them to code-switch, and survive in dual worlds—the world in which they live physically and the world in which their teachers expect them to live. That is a mindset shift. We need educators to change how they see and recognize culture in the world. Part of this process requires you to educate yourself and let the books take you on a journey that will help you better understand cultural realities and close the distance between you and your students.

Design Your Own Professional Development

If your school or division does not provide culturally responsive professional development, there are steps you can take today to ensure that your professional growth continues! Explore the following self-driven professional development options. Start by selecting your immediate area of focus. Then, explore one or more avenues to strengthen your practice as an educator.

What is your focus?	Explore these avenues to professional growth!
Finding opportunities within my school	• Find an accountability partner. This could be a colleague in your school building or district who is interested in culturally responsive teaching or equity. Keep each other accountable for reflecting on your practices and engaging in professional growth.
	• Have you read any good books lately? Consider starting a book club! Ask colleagues in your school or division if they would be interested in participating in an equity-themed book study.
Learning from leaders in the field	• Start building your library. Expand your collection of professional books by exploring topics such as equity, bias, and culturally sustaining practices.
	• Subscribe to podcasts and blogs. Embed time in your daily or weekly routine to engage with the content.
	• Attend virtual summits and webinars. Many of these events are free or inexpensive. Check with your school or division to see if they will support your attendance by covering related costs or awarding professional learning points.

What is your focus?	Explore these avenues to professional growth!
Building a digital professional learning network (PLN)	• Join or start a Facebook group. Educators are increasingly using social media platforms like Facebook to connect with colleagues who share similar passions. This is a great way to engage in discussions, share and receive resources, and expand your circle!
	• Join or start a group chat on Voxer. Voxer allows groups of individuals to participate in a conversation using real-time voice messaging. Enlarge your PLN by expanding the conversation!
	• Participate in Twitter chats. Twitter chats anchor a facilitated conversation using a hashtag. Often, Twitter chats occur at a particular time on a specific day of the week. Browse Twitter for hashtags that support your professional learning goals.
Strengthening my local community connections	• Attend local Edcamps. An Edcamp is a professional learning experience driven by educators and implemented by educators. There are no presenters or presentations at an Edcamp; participants build the learning schedule organically! This is a great way to connect with colleagues in your community who have similar passions, values, experiences, or goals.
	• Connect with local civic groups. Keep in mind that there are many organizations supporting equity work within our communities that are not directly affiliated with schools. Explore the learning opportunities available through community groups that might support your work as an educator.

Conclusion

I want to leave you with some tips that will help you better educate yourself and use that education in your classrooms.

Cultivate your classroom culture. Composing a classroom mantra is a tangible way to help you and your students understand, acknowledge, work toward, and hold each other accountable for the dialogue that guides your classroom.

The next step is the **importance of instructional planning**. As you select the instructional resources and activities that will support the learning experiences in your setting, ask yourself, "Who is seen, and how are they represented? Who is centralized, and who is celebrated?" These questions will help keep you accountable for affirming cultural diversity and adopting an anti-racist lens through your teaching.

You need to have some **feedback strategies**. If we approach feedback as a collaborative construction of knowledge, our goal shifts from one-way communication to a process of listening, sharing, and learning from each other. Whether you are interacting with students, staff, or families, aim to utilize feedback structures and create opportunities for honest dialogue through two-way communication.

Finally, **reflection** is very important because at the end of the day, it's important that you designate a moment for genuine self-reflection. Think about how you showed up during the day. Were you practicing anti-racist practices in your words and actions? Were you solely nonracist? Where can you identify opportunities for yourself to make amends, increase equity in your learning environment, or advocate for greater representation and inclusion?

As you discuss complex notions about race and ethnicity, be willing to learn something new, especially from your students. This might require you to find your own professional development opportunities to increase your knowledge. Be careful, however. Do not rely on another person to teach you everything about their identity. Engage people on their terms and do not expect them to accept the burden of automatically educating you about topics that are unfamiliar to you.

Model Vulnerability and Humility

2020 and 2021 were some rough years for me on a personal level. In 2020, the Leading Equity Center and the podcast really started to take off, and I found myself in a position where I was working two full-time jobs. I am the special education director at my school on the reservation, and I also was basically watching the Leading Equity Center grow into an entity that required that I put in roughly 40 hours a week on top of my daytime job. Obviously, I was working my behind off.

When you start to do a lot of things, that's just the work side. You probably have other responsibilities, such as your family, and you have the mental capacity and energy to maintain all these responsibilities. Some of us finally started to think about what that looks like as an educator while experiencing something like the COVID-19 pandemic. We were all forced to stay at home. We were not able to do the things that we are used to doing. As a result, there were some things that I didn't do well. I'll admit that. The last couple of years have been rough because on the personal side, the family dynamics have changed. I went through a divorce. It was a very stressful time; I'll just put it that way. I'm not going to go into details regarding all the ins and outs of what I experienced. I'm still trying to maintain my sanity, maintain my business, and be the best educator and father that I can be at the end of the day.

The thing about being educators is that we're humans first. What does that mean? It means that we're fallible. Sometimes, we hold our students to certain unrealistically high standards. We expect our students to perform despite everything that they have going on, and we expect them to perform well. We expect them to do all the things that we require of them in an orderly fashion according to our rules and regulations. Sometimes, we forget the social and emotional side of what it means to be a student. Think about what it takes as adults to deal with social pressures, financial constraints, marriage and family challenges, and uncertainties when it comes to dealing with loss and responsibilities. Then, we come to class every day. We come to our schools. We walk in the hallways, and we're supposed to keep a smile on our face. Sometimes, it's difficult.

This chapter discusses how to keep your energy up even when you are facing distractions at home and work. I will discuss ways that you can connect more with your students and the school community by being vulnerable. Sometimes, being vulnerable is complex, and it may make us uncomfortable at times. However, we must show our human side while staying true to our values.

How Can I Smile When My Cup Is Empty?

I live in Idaho. A few years ago, there were quite a few murders of unarmed Black men by the police. I remember coming into work one day feeling isolated, alone, and like I didn't have someone to talk to who could understand what I was experiencing. When Michael Brown was shot and killed, I was a school principal in Oregon and the only Black staff. I remember showing up to work the next day to lead a staff meeting. Initially, I felt like I needed to pretend as if things were normal, but I could sense that they knew I was bothered. I've never been good with a poker face. If I'm bothered, and you know me, you know that something's bothering me. I'm not good with covering that up. I remember sitting there in my staff meeting, and someone asked me, "Are you okay?" I said, "No, I'm not okay."

Even when we are in leadership positions, we're expected to have a certain character, and we're expected to stay positive and never be bothered. We are supposed to be unwavering because we know that folks are looking at us. Our staff depends on us to hold the ship in line as the captain of the school. At the end of the day, we're still human beings. Sometimes, we forget about that. Even when we're in charge of our classrooms, our students are looking up to us, and they expect us to be a certain way. You know what? Life happens.

Last school year, I had a conversation with my former principal, and I said, "Listen, I've been here all school year, but I've been dealing with a divorce. Although I've been physically at this school, I haven't been at the school." By the way, I'm glad that there are a lot more conversations happening regarding mental health. I said, "Look, for my sanity, with everything I have going on in my life, I'm not going to be able to keep this job. I'm not giving the kids the best. I'm not giving the school the best that they deserve right now. I need to choose my sanity, my mental health, over anything else."

I'm a big proponent of the importance of relationships. Connecting with students who have different experiences than us may be a challenge; however, we can form bonds and still stay true to our personality traits. I believe one common denominator through all of that is that all our students can appreciate authenticity.

Students know what's up. If we aren't being genuine or authentic for our students, they recognize that, and I don't think that's going to strengthen any relationship. Being authentic also means that you're okay with being vulnerable. That's part of being authentic. If I'm not willing to show some sort of humility or be vulnerable, my students will not trust me.

We don't have to put on a show all the time. I would just argue that the best way, again, is to show our human side.

We think that because we are adults, we have folks looking up to us, or we're in leadership positions in which we must be an expert. We feel that we must behave and act a certain way.

I want to congratulate the schools out there that are social and emotional learning oriented. They are making sure that emphasis is not extended just to students, but also to staff. I want to recognize principals and superintendents who understand the importance of mental health and the value of taking care of their staff. I believe that a school is a community. It's not just for one person. It's not just for students. It's for families, parents, guardians, community members, faculty, and staff. If you are in a leadership role, you need to be attuned to the emotional needs and stresses of our school's families to ensure the school culture is positive.

The Unintentional Battle Between Us and Them

When we're doing equity work, there never should be an us versus them mindset. Instead, recognize that you are in it together with your school community. Do not be afraid to show your students, your parents, and other stakeholders that you don't know something. Show them that you still are developing your capacity for understanding the experiences your students have at home and at school. Being vulnerable is not the easiest thing for educators to do because we often operate from an authoritarian and classroom leadership perspective.

However, students respect the fact that teachers are unafraid to display their lack of understanding and their willingness to learn from their students. Here are some questions I want you to ask yourself:

- How can I expect students to feel safe to share about themselves if I am not willing to do the same thing?

- Who are people in my life who can serve as accountability partners in my pursuit of an equitable environment?
- Where's a safe space, a system, or resources that will allow me to engage in conversations on how to serve my community more effectively?

Another way that humility can work is by participating in the same activities as your students. If you are having students participate in discussions and activities that require them to share personal stories and understanding, model that same vulnerability by opening yourself up to help students get to know you on a personal level. However, that does not mean that you need to pour your heart out to folks. That's not what I'm saying. What I am saying is I think a student can appreciate hearing you say, "You know what? I'm dealing with some struggles just like your parents, guardians, or you are experiencing. I dealt with something similar when I was your age." I think a student can appreciate that. Again, you don't have to go all into details. They don't need to know everything. Just knowing that there are similarities and some experiences to which we can relate provides a little bit more empathy toward them, and it helps build the connection between your students and you.

Think about vulnerability. It's not just to your students, but it also is important for your colleagues and your peers. George Floyd was murdered during a pandemic, and many people were paying attention. It's not like it was the first time police brutality resulted in the death of unarmed men or women of color. However, when George Floyd's murder happened, people were at home, and they were paying more attention to social media.

Many educators, especially those who are white, reached out to me during this timeframe and said, "Sheldon, I feel like I need to say something, but I don't know what to say. You're a person who I respect, and I value your opinion. I would love to get some of your thoughts about how I can approach this." Any time I get asked for support or my opinion, I always preface my response with the response, "This is my opinion. I do not speak for everybody." I remember helping many people out and providing as many tweets as I could. Again, this tragedy took place in the middle of a lot of personal things I had going on, but I felt that there was a need for me to speak out, and I wanted to support people as much as I could.

I know a lot of people are very uncomfortable with having conversations about race. They recognized that even though they were uncomfortable, they needed some help. It's an honor that folks would reach out to me. I was happy to provide any support that I could, but it takes humility to ask for help. Some of the people who reached out to me were well-known within their industry and field. These were very respected, highly regarded people. It takes vulnerability and humility to reach out to someone and let them know, "Hey, listen, I don't know what I'm doing. I'm supposed to know what I'm doing, but I don't. I'm still trying to figure this out."

The thing about it is we've all been wrong. There's no perfect educator. There's no perfect person. In the experiences we've had and will have in our lives, we understand that make mistakes, and we learn from those mistakes. I always tell people not to dwell on those things. Take them as a learning experience and an opportunity for growth. The decisions and choices we make come from our lived experiences.

Whenever you're reaching out being vulnerable and humble, approach those conversations with the goal of learning and understanding, not persuading or convincing. When I was the principal of a smaller private school, I was the only Black staff member, and my daughter was the only Black girl in the entire school. I remember a new Black family who was interested in our school, and they had a son. I remember listening to the parent, as she told me,

"I want my son here because this school has a Black principal. I want my child to see this." I, on the other end, was excited, because I was happy to see a Black family, and I was very happy to see a young boy with whom I might have some opportunities to connect, so they enrolled their child in my school.

It wasn't long before this kindergartner had some challenges. A kid in the first grade started calling him "Chocolate Boy," but because he was a kindergartener, he didn't realize what was happening. He didn't try to stop it. Somehow, I was notified that this child was being called "Chocolate Boy." I honestly didn't know what to do. This was years ago. This was before I started the podcast. This was before I got into this work. I felt some political pressure as the only Black person. I already felt like being who I was and how I identified cause me to have to work twice as hard, and I had to prove that I was worthy of being in this space. Dealing with a racial slur or racial issues during a community who probably never felt or had to think about the type of things that I (and this young boy and his family) had to consider was a difficult dynamic. This incident happened on a Friday, and rather than immediately addressing it, working on it, or doing anything about it, I didn't do anything. I figured that I would spend the weekend thinking about what to do next, how to handle it, and how to address it.

On Monday morning, I got a call from the parent. She said, "My son's been called Chocolate Boy, and I heard that you knew about this. I'm disappointed that you didn't even at least call us to talk to us about it. You did nothing. I felt let down. We brought our child here because we thought he would be safe and secure because our kindergartner has a principal who looks like him." I was disappointed as an educator, a school leader, and a person of color, and I felt bad. I said, "Listen, I'm sorry. You're right. I didn't do anything about it. Honestly, I didn't know what to do."

I know I didn't handle this right. Now, here's the thing. It takes a lot to say, "You know what? I was wrong." It also takes a lot to grow and say, "Never again." Ever since that day, any time I hear about situations in which a student is dealing with challenges such as bullying, racism, prejudice, or oppression, I make it my business to address these things immediately. I at least notify the parents or the persons involved and say, "Listen, I don't have a decision right now, but I just want to make sure that you're aware that we are working on this." That was a lesson that I learned. The parent was disappointed that nothing was done, and I knew that I should have handled the situation differently.

I don't dwell on what happened with that lapse in my judgment, and I don't wrestle with it either. I take the situation as a learning experience and an opportunity for my own personal growth as an advocate. There is no such thing as the feeling that you have arrived, and you are an equity expert. I do not believe in that. Equity is such a broad term. I don't believe that there's a degree or level of mastery of equity because there's so much to it. There are so many things that I never will experience when it comes to equity.

I'm a cisgendered, heterosexual man, so there are going to be a lot of challenges that I will never experience. I never will know what it's like to feel discriminated as a member of an LGBTQ+ community. I'll never know what it's like to feel any sort of gender bias as a woman, and I don't have to worry about walking down the street in the dark by myself for my safety most of the time. That's not something that I consider. Even though I may not be able to relate to certain situations that my students are facing, I can display empathy and listen to their concerns. But this may mean that I have to be vulnerable and remind individuals of my ignorance around topics that I am trying to understand.

When it comes to humility, we also must consider the importance of how things make us uncomfortable sometimes. When you're reflecting on and learning from your mistakes, it's not the easiest thing to do. In fact, it's pretty tricky, and it even might hurt your pride a little bit, especially during those first few times that you make mistakes. However, these conversations are all about making us uncomfortable. We must be able to say, "Hey, I need your help" or "Hey, I made a mistake."

Sometimes, we have to try to figure out ways to get comfortable, and I've been shifting away from the conversation about being comfortable with your discomfort. For me, it's more of the importance of being confident in your approach. The more you build and take the time to educate yourself, the more experiences that you have. You will be more aware when it comes to being an equity advocate, and that will make you more confident to build your knowledge. However, when it gets uncomfortable, that's the time when we need to stand in it. Those are the moments when we need to be confident. As you become closer and closer to being a more equity-focused and equity-minded individual, it's not going to be easy. It's not supposed to be easy. It's going to be hard work. However, stay the course. Model your own vulnerability and humility. Be authentic for your students, their families, and the community. Be authentic as you develop your skills on this equity journey. Sometimes, we get defensive when we get called out for things, especially when they're unintentional. Be okay with it. Be open and embrace it.

Never forget that you don't get to decide if it is valid or not when others are upset. You don't have the power to determine if their feelings are justified. Respect the experiences of others. What if something that you said seems to rub me the wrong way? In that case, there is a historical context that we need to understand, and there is my lens—a lens that is different than yours because of my experiences, my cultural identity, and, yes, my own privileges and biases.

I had a colleague who posted a message on social media. It said, "For years, I thought that if people of color would just comply or never do the crime, they wouldn't experience the things they experience. There's no real reason for them to complain; it's their own fault that they're in these situations."

I remember him following that up with this statement. "Well, I've changed my stance. I've been fighting it for a while, but I have seen some things throughout the United States historically, and now, I realize things are happening that are beyond people of color's control. Just because I've never experienced these things, I've never actually faced this for myself, I can look at it from a different perspective. I've been in situations where there were four of us, three people of color and me, and I saw how the police treated them versus how they treated me. I've seen these things firsthand. Now I've changed my stance." That's the growth that we want to see, and that is why I fight so hard for equity.

Be willing to acknowledge that you might be wrong! Understand that we all have implicit biases that can misinform how we perceive the world. Approach the conversation with the goal of learning and understanding, not persuading or convincing.

Get Comfortable with Discomfort

Reflecting on your mistakes and learning from them is not the easiest thing to do. In fact, it's pretty tricky, and it even might hurt your pride a little bit, especially those first few times. However, that is what these conversations are all about. We are changing our vastly differing perspectives based on new knowledge. It's going to get uncomfortable, but it's worth it.

I've talked about race, and I like to have fun, so I might crack a joke here and there that makes you uncomfortable, but these are things that we need to discuss. It's okay to be uncomfortable. I want you to be uncomfortable because when you start to get uncomfortable, that means you're asking questions like, "What are some next steps? What's this feeling that I have?" Those kinds of things start to happen, and you start to think, *What can I do? What can I change because I want to have these conversations? I'm uncomfortable, but I must push through it.*

For some of us, simple tasks such as turning the radio on, finding a radio station that plays the kind of music we like, or turning on the television and confidently knowing that we can find a channel or a show in which our racial identity is represented positively is important. We want to know that we are going to see representatives of our race. We can live in the neighborhood that we choose. More than likely, there are going to be people who look like us. Our supervisor more than likely will look like us. These everyday experiences provide us with comfort, and now, I am asking you to get uncomfortable. I want to build your racial stamina.

Let's just say you have a 20-minute conversation in your classroom that has to do with race. If you are not a person of color, when faced with that idea, you're like, "Well, I don't want to do that." Just having the privilege of being able to say, "I don't want to do that," and saying, "I'm not going to engage in this conversation" is another level of privilege that you have in a white-dominated society.

For many people of color, that's not an option; that's something that we deal with daily. We don't get to pick and choose. I don't go home and take my Blackness off and go to sleep. I can't do that. I'm Black when I go to sleep, and I'm Black when I wake up. That is not a comfort level that I get to pick and choose.

Here's the bottom line. You are going to be uncomfortable while doing this work. If you aren't, then you aren't doing it right. There will be things that make you want to end the discussion, get defensive, or just walk away. Those moments are the most significant opportunities for your own growth.

I implore you to have these conversations, and when you start to feel uncomfortable and those flight responses start to kick in, sit in it. Take it in. Really think, *Why am I reacting this way? What experiences in my life have put me at this point, and what experiences does the person to whom I am talking to bring to the table? How can I respect this person's experiences and use this conversation for my own growth? What is the historical context at play here? How can I be a better advocate to the students and community that I am serving?*

Because concepts of race, culture, and identity are complex and deeply personal, they often bring feelings of discomfort. Many of us enjoy talking to our students about the latest movies we saw over the weekend, music, activities, and events in our communities. Yet, racial issues such as police brutality and xenophobia are avoided at all costs. Whether we address these issues, our students are thinking and talking about these issues. We cannot avoid these conversations because they make us uncomfortable. Get comfortable with your discomfort, and do not use it as an excuse to avoid engaging with people who are different from you.

Staying True to Your Values

How can we, as educators, keep ourselves accountable for acting in accordance with our values? This resource presents three simple steps that you can follow to align your practice with your core values.

- **Affirm your mission daily**—Before you can hold yourself accountable for acting in accordance with your values, you must be crystal clear about what those values are. Begin with the end in mind and outline your vision for yourself, your students, and your school community. Consider the traits that feature prominently in your vision and use these values to craft a mission statement that reflects your personal role in making this vision come to life! Affirm this mission each morning to set the tone for your day.

- **Select an accountability partner**—An accountability partner should be a person who is well acquainted with your mission and values. While the person does not have to share all your values, they must be able to support you by offering honest feedback and reflections. Consider selecting an accountability partner who understands the principles of equity and the value of teaching through a culturally diverse lens. Set aside time to talk with this person regularly about your dilemmas and experiences. Keep in mind that technology and social media will allow you to connect with a colleague in a different district, state, or country!

- **Revisit your values often and loudly**—One of the best ways to hold yourself accountable for operating in alignment with your values is to make those values known to others! Think about the 30-second elevator pitch that you use to introduce yourself when you meet someone new. Does this introduction express your values? Make an intentional choice to infuse your core values into the world's understanding of who you are. In addition, keep yourself open to interactions and experiences that might shift your values. As the world becomes more complex and our communities become more diverse, it is likely that your perspective will evolve as it is enriched by new voices!

Conclusion

I've learned over the years that it's unfair to expect our students to open up to us about what they have going on in life if we are unwilling to share about our experiences as well. Take the time to let your students know that you may be facing challenges as well. You don't always have to go into details and share the full extent of your situations. It's helpful to express your discomfort and work through that.

I have had many students share with me situations that they had going on at home. While going through some of my most challenging moments, I was able to find support from my students and colleagues to help me through my tough situations. I hope that you can do the same thing.

9

Recognize How to Build on Students' Assets

"Competency precedes confidence."

—Zaretta Hammond

Oftentimes, educational interventions focus on the deficits of the children versus their strengths. We need to look at what our students know *first* and how they see themselves in the lessons we provide for them. This chapter will equip you with strategies for asset-based pedagogy. When we acknowledge that we know the strengths of our students, they will be confident in learning from us as educators.

This chapter is all about asset-based teaching. I will discuss what it means to view the individuality of students and their talents as assets. Rather than focusing on students' deficits such as lower reading scores, learning loss, and statistics, we can embrace students where they are and build from there. I also will discuss teaching strategies for asset-based pedagogy.

Moving from Deficit-Based to Asset-Based Teaching

Let's talk about what it means to move from deficit to asset-based teaching. Traditionally, youth from marginalized communities tend to be viewed through a lens of what they don't have. We might consider the parents' or guardians' level of education, the students' proficiency in speaking English, or their reading or math levels. As a result, many educational interventions are focused on the areas of deficiency, so the approach focuses on the students' lack of language, grit, or whatever it is that we want to increase to improve achievement.

It's a "Let's give them what they don't have" mentality.

This is working from a deficit lens. It's even built into our school systems sometimes. For example, we use the term *English language learners* to address students who are not proficient in English. However, if we compare that to a term like *emergent bilinguals* or *emerging multilingual students*, we recognize those children who speak a language other than English in their home, and we acknowledge that they will be bilingual/multilingual. Currently in America, being able to speak multiple languages but not being able to speak English "well" is looked at as a deficit.

Components of Asset-Based Pedagogy

Asset-based pedagogy has various components. One is the knowledge teachers have that informs what they believe and what they do. There is research that indicates that teachers who learn about the multicultural education movement as well as civil rights, law, and history have a much deeper understanding of achievement disparities, which ensures that they don't blame students. Educators with a higher understanding of multicultural education strive to assist students in reaching their full potential.

The second component of asset-based pedagogy is knowing how to build on students' assets, and to do that, we need to know who our students are and how they might be missing from the curriculum. This includes asking questions like, "Can my students see themselves in the books and in the subjects taught?"

Asset-Based Mindset Anchor Chart

In a nutshell, asset-based pedagogy is the practice, knowledge, and dispositions that view students as having assets to counter the many ways that we tend to see them as having deficits. Let's look at some examples. The following "cheat sheet" supports educators in changing their language as they shift their mindset from a deficit-based approach to a strengths-based approach. Consider how the phrases in the first column may marginalize or denigrate students. Then, reframe your thinking using the phrases in the second column to embrace aspects of students' culture and identity as assets to the learning environment. At the end of the resource, reflect on your own use of language and generate strengths-based alternatives to deficit-based statements.

Instead of asking . . .	Try . . .
"Does your family speak any English at home?"	"What other languages do you and your family speak?"
Instead of saying . . .	**Try . . .**
"You need to write using proper English in this class, not slang."	"Tell me more about why you chose to say it that way."
Instead of saying . . .	**Try . . .**
"You're being too loud."	"Let's figure out the best way for you to share your ideas with the class."
Instead of saying . . .	**Try . . .**
"Sometimes, this skill is just more difficult for girls."	"How might we build on your ability to. . .?
Instead of asking . . .	**Try . . .**
"Why can't you just sit still?"	"I wonder if you could use your energy to help me. . ."
Instead of saying . . .	**Try . . .**
"If you want people to take you seriously, you need to dress more professionally."	"Can you share with me how your clothes reflect who you are as an individual?"

(Continued)

Instead of asking . . .	Try . . .
"Haven't you ever been to a birth-day party?"	"Tell me more about how your family celebrates special occasions."
Instead of asking . . .	**Try . . .**
"Can't your parents help you with your homework?"	"Who do you ask when you need help outside of school?"
Instead of saying . . .	**Try . . .**
"You need to fix your behavior."	To focus on what's working.

A few additional reminders about your students:

- They have unique strengths, passions, and interests.

- They are competent and capable in settings that are important to them.

- They have their own personal powers.

- They have much to offer to other learners and their school communities.

- They are sources for educating others about their communities and cultures.

- They thrive in a climate of differentiated instruction and the universal design for learning.

- Even though they are not marching to the beat of a traditional school design, it doesn't mean they are out of step.

Funds of Knowledge

Moll, Amanti, Neff, and Gonzalez (2009) call this approach the "funds of knowledge."[1] This philosophy values the positives and strengths that students bring into the classroom. Asset-based teaching approaches each student as a whole person, including their culture, home life, prior experiences, and knowledge. This approach has the perspective that all these areas can be brought into the classroom environment.

Advanced Courses

Another example of taking an asset-based approach for our students is through advanced courses and gifted programs. Are students of color receiving the same opportunities to enter these programs as everyone else? Students who have educators who view their abilities as valuable are much more likely to be better achievers in part because with this attitude, the teacher's biases won't interfere with the teacher-student relationship. It is also helpful if a teacher shares a racial or cultural background with the student. However, with a teaching force of more than 80 percent white educators and 51 percent students of color nationwide, there is a huge mismatch between who we're seeing go into the classroom and who they are teaching. If students don't see examples of themselves in their teachers, that's a problem. It's not that they always must have teachers who share their cultural background. Students need to see examples that success is a possibility for them.

Yes, representation in our teaching force is important because understanding lived experiences plays a role in the way we teach. However, representation is not always available. In general, students need teachers who understand their backgrounds including their language and culture and who use this knowledge in the classroom.

Classroom Dynamics

Let's talk about classroom dynamics. Classroom dynamics refers to a system of information in which teachers' knowledge and beliefs inform what they do. Their behaviors and the things they do in a classroom inform what students believe about themselves and about each other. A self-fulfilling prophecy about whether they can succeed or are doomed to fail could be a result of these classroom dynamics. Later in this chapter, I will bring up how biases contribute to students' belief in their own potential. Just living in society, we absorb information about groups of people because of how they're represented or not represented in the media, movies, and books. That influences all of us. Teachers are part of a society flooded with these messages, and those messages tend to be most harmful toward students of color.

Understanding the realities of our students' lived experiences removes the stereotypes and myths associated with them and their social groups. Here are two considerations:

- **Become the example**—As I mentioned earlier in this chapter, traditional approaches to education look at what students don't have, including a stable home, grade-level reading and math skills, and language abilities. Rather than follow the traditional approach, you can become an example by advocating for students who have been labeled by a deficit lens. This can be a powerful and contagious way of changing a school's culture and the way students are talked about at school. When negative conversations occur about a "troublemaker" or English language learner, see these conversations as teachable moments to help your fellow educators look at things differently. Discuss the reality that many of these students have been cheated in our educational system, and the onus to remedy this problem is on us, not the students. Find allies who will share this message and continue to talk positively about students in teacher meetings and informal conversations with your colleagues.

- **Taking an asset-based approach to teaching requires us to disrupt the traditional teaching practices that we have been taught**—In some cases, it may require more education and training on how to embrace the language, customs, cultures, and beliefs of our ever-changing student demographics. For some teachers, it's a journey to undo all the things to which they've been exposed and the beliefs they have about individuals with whom they weren't raised. It can be quite complicated at times, but doing this equity work is not always easy. In your professional setting, help your fellow educators take the journey toward learning and immersing themselves in different literature and really looking at what your student behavior demonstrates. If students are resistant, they're probably telling you that they're in a system that "dehumanizes me." That may be why they're acting out. They are behaving that way not because they are bad students, but because they are demonstrating to the teacher, "I'm objecting to your dehumanization of me because I am a human being, and I deserve respect."

Change the way we see their behaviors. The reason why a student might not be doing the work and the way we talk about students matter. As an equity advocate, you can help spread the word about being positive and seeing the assets in your students, and that can be very contagious.

How Should We Refer to Students Who Are Struggling?

When we say "struggling," we're approaching things from a deficit mindset. A word that we can utilize instead is "striving." Instead of saying the students are not striving or the students are troublemakers or troublesome, say that they are approaching or striving. They're scholars. I've been hearing a lot of conversations centered around learning loss especially during the COVID-19 pandemic.

There's so much emphasis placed on this learning loss. This is the first time that most people have experienced a pandemic. You know how hard it is to try to focus and learn when you don't know necessarily if you have a roof over your head or you're not used to online learning? It is so difficult if you learn better in person with one-on-one support or multitiered systems of support. You learn better that way, and now you're forced to have to do online learning, which essentially is learning on your own. You don't have someone at home helping you.

We have a lot of kids who are resilient and are surviving, but we spend a lot of time emphasizing the importance of test scores. I've seen schools that emphasize social emotional learning put more emphasis on academics and talk more about learning loss. If we're doing social-emotional learning and if we're claiming that we're an SEL school, we need to be doing this with fidelity. Humanize our kids. I don't like to hear the term "learning loss," because that term reflects a deficit mindset. When we talk about the achievement gap, that is a deficit. Let's celebrate our kids from where they are right now. As of today, this is where they are. How do we build?

Additional Asset-Based Instructional Methods

We often view our schools and classrooms through a homogeneous lens, creating lessons and learning plans from a monolingual and monocultural perspective to fit within a standardized curriculum. The compilation of the following teaching strategies will challenge your thinking about the static roles of the "teacher" and "student" and encourage you to prioritize instructional equity. Each of these pedagogies serves to support students interacting with diverse ideas and challenging their thinking in productive ways. Use the following list as a springboard for investigating various teaching styles or pedagogies that may meet the needs of your students:

- **Asset-based pedagogy**—Asset-based pedagogy is a set of practices, knowledge, and dispositions that views students as having assets to counter the many ways that education tends to view them as having deficits. The strength of an asset-based pedagogy is that it approaches students as a whole people, including their culture, their home life, their prior experiences, and their knowledge with the perspective that all of these areas can be integrated gainfully into the classroom environment.

  The knowledge teachers have informs what they believe and what they do. Strive to assist students to reach their full potential. Know how to build on students' assets by knowing who our students are and how they might be missing from the curriculum.

- **Cooperative learning**—Cooperative learning consists of students working together for a duration of time to achieve shared learning goals and successfully complete tasks and assignments.[2] Cooperative learning shifts the role of the teacher and allows students to learn directly from their interactions with one another. The teacher supports or facilitates the collaborative work by helping students establish norms to ensure that all voices are heard and valued.

- **Cultural storytelling**—Cultural storytelling is the practice of inviting students to share their own stories and bring their own cultures into the classroom to enhance the relevance and authenticity of learning. The underlying principle of cultural storytelling is that students will grow academically, socially, and emotionally from being exposed to each other's narratives and identities.

Each of us has a story. Our classrooms are becoming more and more diverse. It's important for students to share their own stories and cultures to get to know one another and help make learning stick. Take an active role in supporting all facets of a student's identity. Students can bring parts of their cultures and parts of themselves into the classroom. Help to reinforce the notion of the whole student. Respect a student's culture and identity. Encourage growth from being exposed to one another. Every culture has its own stories and narratives. Hear from other people who are different from us.

- **Hip-hop education**—Hip-hop education is a style of teaching that integrates the creative elements of hip-hop into the classroom in authentic and practical ways. Hip-hop education invites students to connect with the curricular content on their own cultural landscape by teaching through their lived realities, interests, and experiences. In this way, students are empowered to engage in higher-level thinking skills including social discourse, critical thinking, and media literacy.[3]

- **Performance-based assessment (PBA)**—Performance-based assessments measure students' ability to apply their skills and knowledge by using higher-order thinking skills to complete a process or create a product. Performance-based assessments typically require students to engage in work that is like the skills and processes used by a professional in the field.[4] In contrast to traditional assessment practice or standardized testing, performance-based assessments allow students greater latitude to demonstrate their mastery by leveraging their skills, talents, and abilities.

- **Project-based learning (PBL)**—Project-based learning is a teaching method in which students gain knowledge and skills by working for an extended period to investigate and respond to an authentic, engaging, and complex question, problem, or challenge.[5] Project-based learning allows students to investigate and explore concepts that have meaning to them and empowers them to leverage their voices in service of a real-life problem or community need.

- **Universal design for learning (UDL)**—Universal design for learning is a framework that guides the design of learning goals, assessments, instructional methods, and materials in any content area. UDL calls for educators to provide students with multiple means of engagement, representation, action, and expression. The goal of UDL is to produce learners who are purposeful, motivated, resourceful, knowledgeable, strategic, and goal-directed.[6]

Implementing UDL at Your School

How can building leaders ensure the effective implementation of UDL? The following are several strategies that school leaders can employ in conjunction with division initiatives to support the effective implementation of UDL and promote learning for all students.

- **Locate your school within a system of continuous improvement**—Seek to understand how your school's work fits into a model of continuous growth within your school division. Ensure that your faculty and staff recognize your building's role in supporting the strategic goals of the district.

- **Communicate common values to staff and students**— Identify the core values and ethical principles underlying your district leader's commitment to UDL. Clearly articulate these values to your faculty and staff. Embed them into your school's everyday culture so the building is engaging constantly with the ethical framework that supports UDL.

- **Translate district values into building practices**—As you define how UDL looks within your classrooms, take care to align professional practices with the mission and vision of the school district. Revisit these commitments often and offer teachers and students opportunities to unpack what these commitments mean for their daily experiences in your school building.

- **Expect variability within student populations**—Prepare faculty and staff to expect variability within student populations as a normal aspect of teaching and learning. Be proactive by supporting teachers in crafting powerful strategies to ensure that all learners' needs can be met.

- **Articulate clear goals, but stay flexible in your approaches**—Be clear about your goals for both students and staff while allowing for flexibility in approaches. Establish clear expectations about what individuals in your learning community should know and be able to do. Affirm multiple means of reaching these goals and provide equitable support to promote success.

- **Get meaningfully involved in professional development**— As you provide your teachers with opportunities for professional development, model the level of engagement you expect to see. Make it a priority to show up and be meaningfully involved in UDL professional learning opportunities in your district.

- **Designate resources for professional growth**—Make professional growth resources available to teachers who are interested in learning more about UDL. This may require you to designate time or money to increase the accessibility of additional resources such as professional texts, workshops, or conferences. Aim to provide educators with a variety of options to pursue their professional growth.

- **Remain responsive to the needs of students**—Implement a multitiered system of support (MTSS) with fidelity. This will ensure that your school has an embedded structure to discuss student data and to develop strategies collaboratively to meet students' needs. A data-driven system of support also will preserve feedback channels that will allow UDL to remain responsive to the emerging needs of learners.

- **Differentiate between UDL and "good teaching"**—Be clear that all individuals can benefit from UDL; UDL is not a practice that targets struggling teachers or underperforming students. Keep in mind that data can often mask gaps in opportunity and achievement. Teachers who can indicate effectiveness by overall assessment scores or samples of student artifacts should not be exempt from the guidelines of UDL.

UDL Lesson Plan Tuning

The UDL Lesson Plan Tuning Protocol allows educators to receive targeted feedback on their plans for teaching and learning as they align with the UDL guidelines. This structured conversation-based protocol is best completed with a small group of educators (four to six) within an environment that promotes collegiality and professional collaboration. It is most beneficial to include educators with diverse backgrounds and perspectives. You may want to adopt the conversation norms provided, or you may want to generate your own norms collaboratively.

Universal design for learning provides multiple means of engagement, representation, and action and expression to produce expert learners who are purposeful and motivated, resourceful and knowledgeable, and strategic and goal-directed.

UDL Lesson Plan Tuning Protocol (45 Minutes)

The goal of this conversation protocol is to promote alignment between a teaching and learning experience and the principles of UDL.

Suggested Conversation Norms:

1. Critique content, not individuals.
2. Offer feedback from a place of kindness and helpfulness.
3. Share responsibility for including all voices.

No one speaks

The presenter speaks

The tuning group discusses

Ask & respond

Everyone discusses

Required Materials:

- Copies of the lesson plan (one per participant)
- Access to the UDL guidelines

1. **Protocol Introduction** (2 minutes)—The facilitator reviews the goals of the protocol and the discussion norms with the group.

2. **Review Period** (5 minutes)—Participants read the lesson plan and review the UDL guidelines. Participants may take notes to identify evidence of UDL within the lesson plan.

3. 👤 **Explanation** (8 minutes)—The lesson plan presenter explains the context, key objectives, and rationale of the lesson. They may also share concerns, fears, or questions about the lesson.

4. 🗣️ **Clarifying Questions** (4 minutes)—Participants may ask clarifying questions to the presenter to understand the intent of the lesson and the implementation of the plan better. Clarifying questions should be factual and require brief answers.

    Examples of Clarifying Questions:

    What is the duration of this lesson?

    Will students work in groups or individually?

    Where is this lesson situated within the unit of study?

5. 👥 **Likes** & **Wonders** (6 minutes)—Participants may share aspects that they like or appreciate about the lesson plan and aspects that they still wonder or have concerns about. *No suggestions should be offered at this time.*

    Guiding Questions:

    (a) Is there a clear alignment between the lesson plan and the guidelines of UDL?

    (b) Does the lesson plan promote learning and engagement for all students?

    (c) Does the lesson affirm every student's unique background and identity?

I like . . .	*I wonder . . .*
Example: I like how you have planned to provide support for students to set and achieve their own personalized learning goals.	*Example: I wonder if students are given sufficient opportunities to activate their background knowledge about this concept.*

6. 👤 **Presenter Response** (4 minutes)—The presenter may address any pressing concerns or wonderings from the Likes & Wonders discussion.

7. 👥 **Feedback & Suggestions** (8 minutes)—Each participant may offer one piece of critical feedback about the lesson plan and its alignment to the UDL guidelines and one suggestion for revising the lesson plan.

    Guiding Questions:

(a) Where does the lesson plan lack alignment with the UDL framework?

(b) Where in the lesson plan are there opportunities for students to be disengaged? What additional components are necessary to ensure student learning?

(c) In what ways does the lesson plan prevent students from being their authentic selves?

I noticed that . . .	**One way to improve this is . . .**
Example: I noticed that students who speak English as a second language may require additional support to access complex texts.	Example: One way to improve this is to spend some time clarifying vocabulary and illustrate concepts through multiple media such as graphics and video.

8. 👤 **Reflection** (5 minutes)—The lesson plan presenter reflects on the feedback they have received. They may choose to reflect on how their lesson plan might evolve as a result of this feedback. Participants listen silently.

9. 🗘 **Debrief/Closing the Loop** (3 minutes)—Reflect on how the process worked. What went well? What could be improved? How successfully did you adhere to the protocol norms?

Conclusion

Asset-based pedagogy is the view that students bring assets to the classroom as opposed to the view that students come to the classroom with deficits or voids that we, as educators, need to fill. Students of color who are recognized by their teachers for their assets are more likely to be referred to accelerated academic opportunities such as the gifted and talented program, and they are more likely to be successful academically. Fostering student success is about understanding, appreciating, and incorporating students' lived experiences. Students need to see examples of themselves in the content that is presented to them in class to illustrate that there is a possibility for them to achieve.

Ask yourself:

- How can you advocate for students who have been given labels?
- How can you use these conversations as teachable moments?
- How can you revamp your conversations?
- What types of deficit-based language have you heard?
- Do you have allies in this work? If not, how can you gain allies in this work?
- As an equity advocate, how have you helped, or can you help to change the conversation to a strengths-based dialogue?

When students' identities, languages, and cultures are suppressed to showcase the dominant culture's way of life, it marginalizes and devalues their self-worth. Instead, we need to refrain from pushing our students to reach the level of what society has viewed as acceptable and embrace the uniqueness that students bring to the table and the ways they can be themselves and still achieve success.

Asset-Based/Culturally Diverse Lesson Planning

How to Use This Template:

How diverse is the student population at your school? Relying on just textbooks that do not present a culturally diverse perspective of the world is problematic. Use and adapt this lesson plan template to craft learning experiences that intentionally consider, embrace, and appreciate the cultural diversity of your classroom, school, and community.

How do I plan with cultural diversity in mind?	Culturally Diverse Planning: a lesson plan template that educators can use to craft learning experiences that intentionally consider the cultural diversity of their classroom, school, and community.

Teacher:	Date(s):	Subject / Course:

Learning Outcomes
What do I want my students to learn or be able to do?

Success Criteria
How will students know when they have been successful?

Community Connections
What groups, resources, or individuals might support my students' learning?

Materials and Resources:

↑ _____

↑ _____

↑ _____

↑ _____

↑ _____

↑ _____

☐ All students have equitable access.

☐ Resources reflect my students' backgrounds and identities.

☐ Resources expose my students to new perspectives and ideas.

☐ Materials support independent thinking and exploration.

Teaching and Learning Strategies:
Check off all that apply:

☐ Asset-Based Pedagogy

☐ Cooperative Learning

☐ Cultural Storytelling

☐ Hip-Hop Education

☐ Performance-Based Assessment

☐ Project-Based Learning

☐ Universal Design for Learning

Engage
How will I use my knowledge of my students' identities and interests to spark their curiosity about the content?

Critically Consume
How will my students access and interact with the information they need to be successful?

Explore
How will my students apply their learning in an authentic context?

Creatively Assess
How will I empower my students to demonstrate their learning and showcase their strengths?

Debrief
What opportunities will I provide for my students to reflect and provide feedback on their experience as learners?

Enrich
* How will I provide enrichment opportunities for students?
* How will I ensure that students have equitable access to these opportunities?
* What additional resources or assistance might I need?

Support
* How will I identify students who need additional support?
* How will I ensure that this support is equitable?
* What additional resources or assistance might I need?

Educator's Reflection
- *To what extent were students able to meet or exceed the learning outcomes?*
- *To what extent did all learners receive equitable access to resources, support, and enrichment opportunities?*
- *To what extent were students empowered to make choices about their own learning?*
- *Would a different teaching and learning strategy have been more appropriate for this lesson?*
- *How might you alter your practice to embody teaching through a culturally diverse lens?*

- Authenticity, relevance to lived experience
- Mirrors and windows
- Learning strategy
- Hook/interests
- Accommodations and enrichment opportunities
- Materials and supplies, with equitable access
- Empowers students to be independent thinkers
- Empowers students to learn from each other
- Personalization
- Pacing and higher level thinking
- Exploration
- Feedback

Classroom Resources and Curriculum Audit

How to Use This Resource:

Consider the following components of your classroom environment and your taught curriculum. Reflect on the extent to which each of these components affirms your students' backgrounds, identities, and interests.

Classroom Resources

Classroom Resources	To a great extent	To some extent	Not at all
Classroom Decorations			
To what extent are my classroom decorations uniquely personalized by my students?			
To what extent can my students see their interests and identities reflected in my classroom decor?			
To what extent does my classroom decor offer my students windows into cultures and experiences that are different from their own?			
To what extent do my classroom decorations affirm my students' cultures and backgrounds?			
Learning Tools and Resources			
To what extent do all my students have equitable access to the materials and supplies available in my classroom?			
To what extent does my classroom offer the resources and supplies necessary for my students to feel safe and valued?			
To what extent do the materials and resources available in my classroom empower all my students to become independent thinkers?			
To what extent are the rewards and/or incentives I offer my students reflective of their interests?			

Classroom Resources	To a great extent	To some extent	Not at all
Classroom Libraries			
To what extent can my students see their identities reflected in the texts in my classroom library?			
To what extent does my classroom library offer students windows into cultures and experiences that are different from their own?			
To what extent does my classroom library push students to engage in higher-level thinking regardless of their culture, interests, or reading level?			
To what extent does my classroom library empower students to choose texts and stories that are interesting to them?			
To what extent do the texts in my classroom library represent the authentic experiences of individuals from culturally diverse backgrounds?			
Curriculum			
Curricular Texts			
To what extent can my students see their identities reflected in the curricular texts?			
To what extent do the curricular texts offer my students windows into cultures and experiences that are different from their own?			
To what extent do the curricular materials support my students in becoming independent thinkers?			
To what extent is the curriculum relevant to my students' lived experiences?			
Topics			
To what extent are my students afforded opportunities to personalize the topics they explore to meet curricular objectives?			
To what extent are the topics represented in the curriculum aligned with my students' backgrounds and interests?			

Curriculum

Pacing

To what extent does the curriculum pacing support my students in becoming independent thinkers?

To what extent does the curriculum pacing allow all my students to engage in higher-level thinking, regardless of their cultures or backgrounds?

Learning Strategies

To what extent do the learning strategies I use to support my students in mastering the curricular objectives allow all my students to engage in higher-level thinking?

To what extent do the learning strategies promoted in my classroom support my students in becoming independent thinkers who value diverse perspectives?

To what extent are students empowered to explore their interests through the learning strategies prioritized in my classroom?

Learning Products and Assessments

To what extent do my content assessments require my students to engage in higher-level thinking, regardless of their backgrounds, cultures, or identities?

To what extent are my students given opportunities to personalize the learning artifacts they produce?

To what extent are the learning artifacts required in my curriculum representative of the world beyond school?

Feedback and Support

To what extent are my students given the opportunity to choose the method by which they receive feedback?

To what extent am I able to support all my students in engaging in higher-level thinking regardless of their cultures, identities, or backgrounds?

To what extent do the methods of feedback in my classroom empower all students to become independent thinkers who value diverse perspectives?

Notes

1. Moll, Louis C., et al. "Founds of Knowledge for Teaching: Using a Qualitative Approach to Connect Homes and Classrooms." *Theory Into Practice, Volume XXXI*, no. 1, 1992.
2. What is Cooperative Learning, Cooperative Learning Institute, http://www.co-operation.org/what-is-cooperative-learning
3. Sparking Engagement with Hip-Hop | Edutopia, https://www.edutopia.org/blog/sparking-engagement-hip-hop-joquetta-johnson
4. Performance-Based Assessment: Reviewing the Basics | Edutopia, https://www.edutopia.org/blog/performance-based-assessment-reviewing-basics-patricia-hilliard
5. What is Project Based Learning? | PBLWorks, https://www.pblworks.org/what-is-pbl
6. UDL: The UDL Guidelines, http://udlguidelines.cast.org/?utm_medium=web&utm_campaign=none&utm_source=cast-about-udl

Use Social Justice as the Basis for Advocacy

"To say nothing is saying something. You must denounce things you are against, or one might believe that you support things you really do not."

—*Germany Kent*

In addition to teaching, a powerful tool that educators have is advocacy. Many of us recognize policies that need to change at our school. However, our voices are often underutilized for various reasons. Maybe it is because we are afraid of getting pushback for our beliefs, or perhaps we are new to our schools and don't think that it's our place to say anything.

The final step toward addressing educational equity is embracing social justice and advocacy. Equity advocates (see Figure 10.1) are not afraid to challenge and disrupt inequities

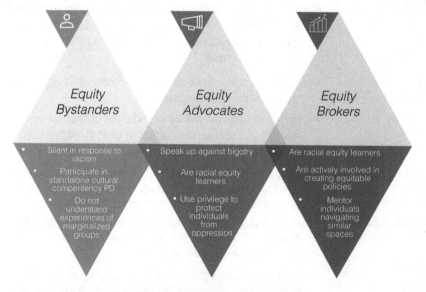

FIGURE 10.1 Which one are you?

taking place at school and in the community. These are the educators who take on comments made against students based on discrimination and prejudice. These are educators to whom students can turn for guidance on how to use their own voice for social justice. These are educators who are not bystanders. They speak up when inequitable practices take place.

How might we, as educators, position ourselves to be equity advocates and equity brokers within educational settings? The following is a progression of mindsets and behaviors that are characteristic of equity bystanders, equity advocates, and equity brokers. Use this progression chart to identify educators who are committed to equity work, or use it to evaluate your own practices in relation to equity.

Equity Bystanders	• Equity bystanders are silent in response to bigotry and racism.
	• While equity bystanders may have participated in one or more stand-alone cultural competency training, they are not engaged in ongoing professional development about culturally sustaining practices.
	• While equity bystanders may share demographic commonalities with members of underserved or underrepresented groups, they do not understand the experiences and patterns that marginalize those groups.
Equity Advocates	• Equity advocates speak up against bigotry and racism when they hear it being perpetuated.
	• Equity advocates are individuals who put themselves in situations as racial equity learners to understand the experiences of the people they serve.
	• Equity advocates use their privilege and power to help protect individuals from the ways that oppression, discrimination, and marginalization operate against them.
Equity Brokers	• Equity brokers are also individuals who put themselves in situations as racial equity learners to understand the experiences of the people they serve.
	• Equity brokers are actively involved in creating equitable and transparent policies within the spaces in which they operate.
	• Equity brokers model and mentor other individuals who are navigating similar spaces or experiences.

When we genuinely care about our students and recognize their needs, we act upon our convictions. To not say anything when we know something is wrong may negatively impact our students and their families. There is no better time than now to practice using our voices to make a change. During these times of uncertainty, we have seen many challenges that our families are facing. Issues such as limited access to Wi-Fi, job uncertainty, and food insecurity are not new. Students working to help supplement their family's income is not a new issue. We can support our families by being a resource for them and helping their voices be heard. That's what being an advocate is all about.

What does it mean to be an advocate? An advocate is someone who acts by speaking in favor of someone, recommending, arguing for a cause, and supporting or defending a position on behalf of others. In education, advocacy may include supporting our students, families, communities, or teachers and staff.

Does this sound like you? Are you someone who takes action to support or defend individuals associated with your school? Let's look at how advocacy can look inside and outside school.

Advocacy Work at Your School

Here are some things you can do at your school:

- **Join equity initiatives**—Get involved in the equity, inclusion, and diversity initiatives in your school or school district. You can amplify your voice as you contribute to committees and groups that share your passion for equity. Be willing to support equity through action. If no equity initiative exists in your school or division, start one!

- **Connect with other antiracists**—Find and connect with other antiracists. Develop a circle of individuals within your community who also care about equity. Seek out educators,

parents, and community members who recognize the inequities taking place within your educational setting. Consider
starting small with a weekly meeting where you can establish a safe space to discuss your concerns.

- **Fill in the gaps produced by racist policies**—Racist policies and ideas negatively impact schools by producing gaps
in resources, curricula, and other areas of students' lived
experiences. Be vigilant about identifying gaps in the system
and create spaces for the necessary work to take place. This
may involve finding ways to meet the physical or emotional
needs of children and promoting an ethic of care.

Advocacy Work Outside of School

In certain contexts, it can be more effective to lead equity as an
individual rather than as a member of an established group.
Consider exploring one or more of the following pathways if you
are seeking to amplify your voice as an equity advocate:

- **Blogs**—Blogging is a simple and effective tool that you can
use to communicate your message to a wider audience. If
you find it natural to express yourself in writing, you may
want to consider this avenue to share your ideas. You can
start a blog entirely on your own, and many platforms are free!

- **Podcasts**—Podcasts, like The Leading Equity podcast, can be
a great way to spread powerful ideas to large groups of listeners.
Podcasting harnesses the power of storytelling to communicate
ideas, and it is becoming a growing trend among professionals
in the field of education. Podcasting also offers opportunities to
partner with collaborators via interviews or co-hosts.

- **Social media platforms**—Educators look to social media
for a wide variety of resources including lesson ideas,

professional learning, and encouragement! If you are a current social media user, consider creating a professional account exclusively for education-related posts so your followers can expect relevant content that is released reliably.

- **School leadership roles**—Some school districts have designated leadership roles specifically for equity work; however, many have not taken this step. Even if "equity" is not in your job title, you can begin incorporating culturally sustaining practices into your existing leadership role. If you do not currently hold a leadership position, you can create your own opportunities to lead! Consider volunteering to facilitate a teacher-led professional development session or open your classroom to visits from your colleagues.

- **Community forums**—Consider the existing avenues for dialogue in your community. Religious, civic, and professional organizations often provide forums for individuals to come together to learn and engage. Stay aware of the local events occurring in your community and contribute your voice whenever possible.

The Three Ps of Advocacy

The success of advocacy often boils down to three Ps. According to Burney & Sheldon (2010), purpose, preparation, and persistence are needed when doing advocacy work.[1]

- **Purpose**—A clear understanding of what is needed begins the process of advocacy for others. Simply making complaints about the daily processes that are in place at your school does not equate to advocacy. Instead, start with some goals. Don't try to address everything that you disagree with at once. Choose something that is the heaviest on your heart and inform yourself of the possibilities of making this change a reality.

- **Preparation**—Depending on your scenario, it is often helpful to have data to support your cause. For example, if you are advocating for a new student organization that supports LGBTQ+ students, you may want to have some feedback from your students. You can provide a survey to students about their sense of belonging or the challenges that they have experienced as students. Ask your students about what they need to feel included in the school culture. This can serve as valuable data to show to your school leaders because the information is coming directly from your students.

- **Persistence**—Building relationships takes time. As you begin to work toward bringing awareness to issues at your school, it is essential that you understand that change rarely happens overnight. Being an advocate requires developing interpersonal relationships and a variety of communication mediums to garner support.

Wherever you are in your journey toward advocacy for equity, remember that creating buy-in is not always easy. Start with your purpose and develop goals that you would like to achieve. Prepare for your interactions with individuals who have the power to enforce change by using student data. Finally, stay persistent with your efforts and recognize that change takes time.

When Your Colleagues Believe That We Don't Have an Equity Problem

"I don't need to learn about equity. I'm pretty confident in my abilities to serve my students." This is a typical response that I get often from educators. I think that we are all in different stages of our journey toward being better advocates for equity. There is always room for improvement.

I constantly am learning new things on my own journey. I started the Leading Equity podcast two years ago, and there has never been an episode with a guest in which I didn't learn something. To say that we have it all figured out means one of two things:

- We genuinely believe that we know all that we need to know, and we don't need to develop our self-awareness.

- We don't like to talk about issues related to race, gender, sexual orientation, etc.

Often, it is the second reason that many educators fail to understand the work that they need to do to create a socially just learning environment.

How do we help others? There are a couple of ways that we can work with our colleagues to help them identify how they may be contributing to systemic inequities.

- **What was school like for you?**—Encourage your colleagues to think about their own educational experiences and identify some of their favorite teachers. Ask them what stood out about the teachers and why they think that they were successful in their teacher's class. Next, ask your colleagues what they think it would take for each of their students to have those same types of memories. As the conversation continues, you may find an opportunity to relate some of the educational experiences that your colleagues had as a student to some of the challenges that students in your school are facing.

- **Ask don't tell**—Rather than trying to convince your colleagues about issues that need to change, try asking them what is holding them back from making a change. Find out what they believe and learn how they see the world. Develop your relationship with them and work toward providing small steps that you are taking in your own position.

Telling staff members that they need to change their ways may warrant pushback especially if they don't want to do it. Instead, we can work on helping our peers see things through their students' eyes by connecting the students' experiences to your peers' background experiences and asking questions about what is holding them back.

As we continue to work on our self-awareness, let's encourage our peers to do the same.

Identifying Equity Issues

As advocates, we may agree readily that equity issues are rife within our system of education. However, pinpointing exactly what those issues are and how they manifest in schools and classrooms can be somewhat more challenging. Inequitable practices often can be subtle, and educators themselves may unwittingly exacerbate inequity through seemingly innocuous behaviors. As you are reading this chapter, you may have questions about how you can identify equity issues. Allow me an opportunity to present several signs that may indicate the presence of an equity issue. While these indicators do not guarantee that a practice or policy is inequitable, they can and should provide you with a starting point to analyze the practice or policy critically and consider the situation carefully.

- **You observe that certain individuals or groups are left out**—A lack of inclusion is a pretty clear indication that a situation, practice, or policy is not equitable. Within a school or classroom, if certain students are excluded from accessing opportunities or resources due to aspects of their identity, background, or culture, those students are not receiving an equitable education.

- **You hear students expressing that something is not "fair"**—Even at a young age, students are keenly aware of what is fair and unfair. Although students may not be able to articulate their feelings about a situation using the language of equity, those feelings of injustice or unfairness are likely a sign that students have experienced or witnessed an inequitable situation.

- **You see that certain individuals or groups are struggling more than others**—Educators constantly are collecting and monitoring student data. When that data indicates that students or groups are struggling to demonstrate achievement in academic or behavioral outcomes, it could be a sign that those students are not receiving equitable support or there are inequitable policies at play.

- **You would classify a choice or behavior as insensitive**—Generally speaking, educational resources tend to default to the dominant culture. The images, examples, and narratives espoused by school systems are often crafted through a lens that centralizes whiteness. Unfortunately, this lens may promote words, actions, and practices within schools that are insensitive to individuals who are not part of the dominant culture. When students' identities, backgrounds, and cultures are marginalized through instruction consistently, they are not receiving an equitable education.

- **You recognize that a policy or decision does not make sense**—You may have heard the phrase, "That's the way we've always done things," used to justify an educational practice or decision. As our schools and communities continue to increase in diversity, you probably recognize that some of these long-standing, traditional practices no longer make sense for the students sitting in our classrooms. Inequitable policies may have been in place for years with little to no revision. One way to start the process of dismantling such policies is by asking why they exist!

- **You witness harm toward an individual or group of individuals**—If any educational practice results in harm toward an individual or a group of individuals, then that practice cannot be equitable. If a student or colleague feels discriminated against or excluded, it is always worth interrogating the practice to determine if it is biased or inequitable.

- **You feel like something just isn't right**—As an advocate, you have probably witnessed or experienced something that just didn't feel quite "right." Equity issues may trigger a general feeling of discomfort that you may not be able to name immediately. In these instances, start by asking questions and see if the answers lead you to the root of the issue.

- **You feel like conditions are stuck or stagnant**—For our practices to be equitable, they also must be culturally responsive. Instructional practices and educational policies should align with the needs of our students and affirm who they are as individuals. If your current context feels stagnant, then you may be dealing with a culture of inequity that discourages student growth and success. Ask yourself what you can do as an educator to advocate for your students' needs and promote a culture of equity and inclusion.

Five Tips for Taking a Stand in the Classroom

Taking a stand can be difficult in any context, but taking a stand in the classroom presents unique challenges for equity advocates. Teachers who work in schools, districts, or communities that cling tightly to traditional practices likely will encounter some resistance as they make changes in support of equity. For instance, many districts have grading policies that impose certain restrictions on the way teachers assess student performance. A curriculum guide that embraces mostly texts that centralize white experiences may marginalize other cultures or themes. If you are a teacher who is ready to take a stand in your classroom, this section of the chapter lists five tips to help you navigate change and promote an equitable learning environment for all students.

Tip #1: Make a Compelling Case

Before making any significant changes to your pedagogical practices or your classroom environment, make sure you are clear about why you are making those changes. While it can be extremely beneficial to learn from other educators, particularly other advocates, keep in mind that not every practice or solution is appropriate for every context. Carefully examine how the change you are considering will benefit your specific students within your school community. Be able to articulate exactly what you hope to accomplish and the outcomes you would like to see.

Tip #2: Know the Rules

The behaviors and practices that take place in schools are often governed by some sort of policy or regulation. As you develop plans to adapt your professional practice, be aware of the policies currently in place that might present barriers or restrictions for your implementation. Is the practice you want to implement allowed? Do you need approval from a department lead, a supervisor, an administrator, or the school board? If you discover that there are existing policies that explicitly prohibit your intended practice, consider following the formal process to initiate an amendment or reconsideration of the policy.

Tip #3: Do Your Research

As an advocate, you exist within a community of other educators who support doing what is best for all students. In many cases, this means someone already has taken the very same stand that you are pursuing! Take the time to find out if any other teachers or schools are using the practice you are interested in adopting. If possible, gather some information about their outcomes and explore their success stories. If there is any research or data related to your goal, become familiar with it.

Tip #4: Assemble Your Network

As you take a stand, it is important to know who supports you and who can advise you. What colleagues, supervisors, mentors, or administrators might be able to help guide you through your journey? Once you have identified your network of support, have a conversation with these individuals about how that support might look. You may need a full-fledged collaborator, or you just may need a listening ear. If you know the type of support you need, do not be afraid to ask for it!

If you have a supervisor or administrator who does *not* support your goal, first try to understand why. Then, work with that person either to build a shared understanding or to establish clear guidelines for how you both will operate respectfully within the context of your work.

Tip #5: Initiate Supportive Dialogue

Finally, but perhaps most importantly, make sure you have developed a plan to communicate changes to your students and their families. Be specific about what they can expect, how they can provide you with meaningful feedback on their experiences, and how you will support them throughout the process. Make sure that they understand why you are adopting a new practice, how it fits into the larger context of the school community, and exactly what you hope to accomplish because of the change. As you keep the safety and success of all students at the forefront of your communication, you likely will encourage others to take a stand right alongside you!

Profile of a Compassionate Leader

Compassion lies at the core of teaching through a culturally diverse lens. Leading with compassion requires intentional reflection and a commitment to continuous growth. The following profile is a snapshot of the characteristics and behaviors of a compassionate leader. Use this profile as a starting point for developing your own vision of the culturally responsive leader you want to be.

A compassionate leader. . .

- Creates an environment that is safe, warm, compassionate, empathetic, and welcoming for all students
- Operates with the intent to support and affirm, not to punish or control

- Mitigates their own implicit biases
- Promotes social-emotional learning and restoration
- Acknowledges disparities and overrepresentation in disciplinary practices
- Strives to build a culture in which students feel loved
- Shapes policies and procedures that promote restorative practices
- Is proactive, not reactive
- Opposes an authoritarian mindset and adopts the mindset of a learner
- Nurtures positive relationships with students, school staff, and the community

What's Next?

What's next? Although the book has ended, the equity work has only begun! You can continue to be a voice in leading equity by intentionally incorporating the following practices into your work as an educator:

Keep learning.
Continue to engage in opportunities for professional growth. If your school division or community does not offer professional development about equity or culturally sustaining practices, expand your professional learning network (PLN) to connect with educators who are leading equity work in their areas. The Leading Equity podcast is a great place to start!

Keep reflecting.
Remember to take time every single day to reflect on your own words and actions as an educator. Implicit bias can show up

in how we interact with students, families, and colleagues! Do your best to remain aware of your biases and be willing to accept responsibility and make amends when your biases cause you to do harm.

Put it into practice.

Show up every day and do equity work! Whether you lead a classroom, a school, or a school district, you play an essential role in leading equity. It will help to find an equity-minded colleague to serve as an accountability partner.

Make an impact.

The only way to improve the educational experiences of all children is to create safe, equitable, and culturally sustaining learning environments. If you recognize an area in your school or community that is not affirming for students from a particular background, take action and change it!

Spread the knowledge.

We are so much stronger together. If you know a colleague who would benefit as much as you did from this book, please share it with them! In this way, we build a powerful network of equity-minded educators who are committed to doing what is best for all students.

Ask yourself:

- If someone asked my students what they liked best about me, would they respond with comments centered around my values of equity and inclusivity?

- Have I missed opportunities to speak up about injustices? What could I do to prepare to respond if inequities take place?

Teachers who have a stronger knowledge of multicultural education as well as civil rights, law, and history have a much deeper understanding of achievement disparities and don't fall into the mindset that blames students for societal and systemic failures. You can be a leader by setting examples for your colleagues; it can be contagious. Examples of warmth and care for students can spread to colleagues who have developed negative views of students and blame them for their lack of success. The more you share with your colleagues, the more opportunities for teachers who are unfamiliar with their own biases to begin their journey of transformation toward an equitable classroom.

Conclusion

Consider all your fellow educators who could benefit from reading this book. As our students navigate the halls and classrooms, you are just one individual who a student will interact with during the day. What good is being an equity-focused educator if you keep everything to yourself? For some students, school is a safe haven. School should be a place where students feel loved and appreciated by all the school staff. Students need to know their worth and that you are willing to support them through your advocacy. Stay on the path of your journey and continue to work toward equity. Doing this work may be challenging at times, but change is not always easy.

Note

1. Burney, Ginny, and Ann Sheldon. "Warrior advocates." *Parenting for High Potential* (2010): 19.

Index